Wolves of Russia

Part Three:

Under the Union Jack

"For our freedom and yours."

(Dyslexia-friendly edition)

Published by Crossbridge Books
Worcester
www.crossbridgeeducational.com

ISBN 978 1 913946 25 8

British Library Cataloguing in Publication Data
A catalogue record for this book is available from the British Library

Wolves of Russia

Part Three:

Under the Union Jack

(Dyslexia-friendly edition)

R M Mace

'The wolf also shall dwell with the lamb,
The leopard shall lie down with the young goat,
The calf and the young lion and the fatling together,
And a little child shall lead them.
The cow and bear shall graze,
Their young ones shall lie down together,
And the lion shall eat straw like the ox.'

Isaiah 11:6-9

CONTENTS: Page:

FOREWORD:

This book is based on the memoirs of a very dear friend of the family who gave his name as: Vincent Viktor Rudolf. Viktor's father died when he was just sixteen, so the early part of this story, told in Part One, though based on his recollections and true accounts, has been reconstructed using historical archives to fill in the 'missing gaps'.

Part Two tells Viktor's own story of deportation to Siberia, escape, and his long walk to Persia. In this volume, Part Three, Viktor recounts his enlistment with the Polish Second Corps, part of the British Eight Army, including the Italian campaign and the historic Battle of Mont Cassino.

Viktor circa 1939

Viktor 2019

Dedicated to the dear memory of my mother, Eileen Margaret Anne Mohr (1931-2022)

"Believe in God and He will be in your heart".

(Viktor November 2022)

PROLOGUE TO PART THREE

"Persia at that time was under British jurisdiction, and into the country were arriving hundreds of Polish prisoners, either escaping from labour camps like me or military prisoners of war, and later, through negotiations being carried out by Polish Generals Anders and Sikorski, it was agreed that the Russian authorities would allow as many Poles as they could to make up an army, to be used to fight against Germany.

As Russia had not got the resources to equip and train these people, it was agreed that the United Kingdom would do so and attach the group to the British Eighth Army. Thus, the Polish Second Corps was established. General Anders was released from the Lubyanka Prison in Moscow to form the newly organised Polish Corps, and thus he travelled to Persia, together with the balance of the Polish Army already imprisoned in Russia.

At this time, the Polish authorities were enquiring as to the whereabouts of 25,000 Polish officers who had not yet joined this group. Stalin indicated that he was looking into the matter, although he already knew that these officers had been murdered by the Russians in the forest at Katyn.

There were several camps in Persia accumulating these groups of Polish Army prisoners of war as they were arriving, and I was sent to a camp in Pahlevi, where I hoped to be accepted into the British Army."

PART THREE

UNDER THE UNION JACK

Viktor's Commemoration badge of the Polish Second Corps

CHAPTER 22

PERSIA (1942)

I don't remember how long I was in the hospital, but I was gently nursed back to health. I was still weak and small for my age but still hoped to enlist with the other Poles into the Polish division that had been organised by General Anders, under the command of the British Army. From the hospital I was sent to a camp on the beach of a town called Pahlevi, on the south-western coast of the Caspian Sea, that had been set up by the British, with the agreement of the Russians who had occupied that part of Persian territory.

It was the end of March, and the ground was wet from melted snow and frequent rain. Thc British had hired accommodation in buildings by the harbour, but since they were expecting very large numbers of Polish soldiers to come by ship from Russia, they had set up a camp on the beach on the west side of the town's Boulevard. As the poor condition of the new arrivals became apparent, the camp officials set up what they called a 'dirty' camp on the beach west of the town where people were disinfested. They were then given clean clothing and sent to a clean camp on the east of the harbour.

The British had set up their headquarters in the Grand Hotel and the Polish evacuation staff were in buildings on the edge of the harbour. Between the two, the Russian HQ and Russian barracks were based. I found the presence of Russian military and NKVD unnerving, but thoroughly enjoyed being able to walk almost unrestricted through parts of the town where the locals had set out their wares for sale. The large buildings in the town were elegant and the roads were proper asphalt. The shop windows were filled with all sorts of things beautifully displayed.

Having known such long periods of starvation, the sight of so much food was a shock to the senses. The smell of the bakery and the Persian flat bread mingles in my memory with the sight of basket loads of eggs, fresh fish, bunches of radishes, and piles of juicy soft fresh fruit – oranges, lemons, bananas, figs, and dates. We ate mutton and rice, dried fruit, bread with margarine, biscuits, and drank tea. Some of the locals were selling a cheap alcoholic drink, and a few of the men tried it but were soon warned off by the medics when they found, that when drunk in excessive quantities, it was causing the men to go temporarily blind. I kept well clear of the stuff.

To get from one side of the harbour to another you had to cross two bridges over small rivers that flowed into the harbour. At one end of the bridge stood a Russian soldier in his helmet, baggy trousers tucked into high boots, and with his long bayonet fixed in place; at the other end stood an Indian soldier from the British Army, dressed in clean khaki shorts and jacket, an elegant turban, and a neatly trimmed moustache and beard on his impassive face. It was one of those surreal moments that etches itself in memory like a picture postcard.

I had arrived in Persia with no papers; I had no means of proving my identity or my age. I guessed that I would be too young to join the regular army, so I told them I was older than I was, and was accepted into a junior group, the cadets, and was drafted into a unit where I was given the job of camp barber. Someone had to do the job and they decided it would be me. A rather brusque fellow took me to a small tent where there was a chair and a table with a small shaving mirror, a comb, and a pair of sharp scissors laid on top.

"Right, you watch while I cut someone's hair and you can see how it's done," he barked. I nodded dumbly, wondering how long it was going to take me to learn this job; I had never cut anyone's hair before and had hardly paid much attention when my own hair had been cut in the past. The first recruit came in and sat in the barber's chair looking relaxed, and probably looking forward to finally getting rid of the long hair. The barber combed and snipped in rapid expert movements as the hair was cut and shaped. Then he handed the comb and scissors to me.

"See how I've done it? That's how you have to do it with all the recruits," he said with a smirk that conveyed the impression that he was quite sure that I would not be able to demonstrate the same skill without any proper training and he found it amusing. He handed me the comb and scissors and told me to get on with it. I remembered from home how the barber had twiddled his scissors in his hands, and so, with trepidation, I twiddled my scissors reassuringly as my first customer entered the tent. The soldier looked around the small tent as if expecting to see someone else, and then looked me up and down.

"You look far too young to be a barber," he said doubtfully, "have you had proper training?" he asked with evident suspicion.

"You will have to wait and see," I replied wondering what the outcome of this venture would be. At first, I tried to use the comb in the same way as the real barber had, but it just seemed to get in the way. Instead, I combed the hair and then put the comb down on the table and used my fingers to gather small tufts of hair to cut. I became absorbed with cutting chunks of hair, listening to the unfamiliar sound, and trying to cut in straight lines to keep it even. It seemed to take ages to try to get the edges straight; I just kept cutting and cutting, a little bit here and a little bit there. When I had finally finished and stood back to look at my work, I could see that the results were terrible. The poor chap saw the look on my face and snatched up the mirror. He gasped and then almost howled with rage, slamming the mirror on the table, and grabbing me around the throat as if to strangle me.

"You're a butcher not a barber!" he yelled at me, "I'll have to wear my cap for a month to hide what you've done to me." The rumour went around camp that the barber was really a butcher, and nobody would come to me. I couldn't believe that these men, who had endured so much, could make such a fuss about their hair. Of course, if the sergeant sent them to me for a haircut, there was no alternative and I had to do it.

Sometime later, a very nice lady, who had been a hairdresser before the war, showed me how to improve my handiwork.

"Can't you be the barber and do this job?" I pleaded, "I'm getting a really bad reputation in the camp; you should hear the verbal abuse I get."

"You'll soon get the hang of it," she said encouragingly, "besides, I don't want to risk picking up something nasty from the lice, or from the severe skin conditions that some of the men have, caused by I don't know what," she said, the disgust barely concealed in her voice. The hairdresser refused to take over from me, but she was right, and I soon did get the hang of it, just as we were moved on to another camp.

Every day, trucks were transporting soldiers and recruits to new camps so that there was a constant stream of evacuees leaving Pahlevi as well as arriving. The ships transporting the soldiers, and later civilians as well, were often too big for the narrow entrance to the harbour, so the passengers, were transferred to smaller boats before being able to disembark. They arrived at all hours, sometimes in total darkness. The evacuees arriving from the port of Krasnovodsk in Soviet Russia had endured horrendously over-crowded conditions without food, water, or sanitation. We heard that conditions in Russia had been terrible, and many had died even before reaching the port from diseases such as typhus that was rife in the Polish camps. Some died on the crossing, and some even died after their arrival, often from overeating or from eating food that was too rich for their starved stomachs like the mutton that was provided unwittingly by the British. I knew all too well what that felt like.

I was moved to a new camp before most of the transports arrived and only learned later some of the horror stories of what people had endured on their journeys to Persia. This had followed the Russian so-called 'amnesty' granted to the Polish people who had been taken captive. The journey by truck from Pahlevi to the next camp via Hamadan was organised by the British, but the drivers were local Persians.

Whichever route you took south from the Caspian Sea would take you over mountain ranges. We were loaded into the back of an old Russian truck. At first, the road led through a beautiful landscape, full of greenery, with early flowers, vineyards, and rice fields. In the distance we could see the Elburz Mountain range covered in vegetation with snow still lingering on the peaks. As we drove up, the landscape changed, the vegetation thinned, and the ground became hard rock. The serpentine roads wound their way steeply up and were mostly wide enough for only one truck, with occasional passing places. The hair-pin bends were hair raising events; one side of the road fell away and there were no safety barriers to help prevent vehicles going over the edge and plummeting into the ravines below. Leaning over a few of the other men and lifting the canvas flap, I had a clear view below of small olive groves and fruit trees dotted around tiny houses. The view of the mountains was incredibly beautiful, and I feasted my eyes on the majestic landscape.

As we swung around yet another tight bend, we could hear the sound of tyres slipping on gravel and held our breath as the truck skimmed the edge of the road. But the driver pulled sharply into the middle of the road even though I was sure that one wheel had been momentarily hanging in the air. The soldier sitting next to me swore.

"These Persian drivers! He's probably drunk; it's the only way they can find the courage to drive on these treacherous roads," he said angrily.

The downhill journey was even more frightening as we descended into the valley. At first, I couldn't understand why the truck was moving so fast and then jerking as it slowed on the bends.

"Listen!" said one of the men near the front of the truck. "I can't hear the engine," he cried out in bewilderment.

"Our maniac driver must have switched off the engine to conserve fuel. He must be relying on the brakes for speed control, and who knows how long they will hold out," shouted another, the disbelief making his voice rather high pitched. This was followed by a silence in which we all sat hoping that the brakes wouldn't fail, but nobody dared express their thoughts aloud. I remember thinking how ironic it would be if, having survived all that we had endured since the invasion of Poland, we were to be killed by falling into a ravine. Later we heard that there were indeed incidents of trucks failing to negotiate curves when relying just on brakes; they went off the side of the road and over the precipice with no survivors. We finally reached the next camp exhausted but heartily relieved to have made it in one piece.

Thankfully, I was given a different job at this camp. Perhaps my reputation had gone before me, at any rate, they didn't want me as a barber. Instead, I was taken to the first-aid tent.

"Here's your first-aid box," I was told, and looked inside. All I could see were aspirins and plasters.

"Is that it?" I asked doubtfully. It was.

"Look, you aren't qualified. You can treat people with headaches or cuts and bruises. If anyone comes along who you think is really ill it will be your job to book them in to see a doctor," was the reply. I felt like a doctor's receptionist, or maybe even the camp nanny, and it wasn't long before I was heartily fed up with my job and applied for a transfer to military school although I was still in the junior army unit.

Like so many others, the time I had spent in Siberia was time that I had missed in education. In all the Polish camps that had been set up in Persia, there were schools for all levels. By this time, the camps were filling up with civilian refugees from Russia that had been able to attach themselves to Anders' Army. There were whole families, and remnants of families, that had survived, as well as countless orphans. There were vast numbers of women, and the children who were too young for military service were provided with education by the army. Some families and children were sent as far as India to continue their education. This option was offered to me, but I wanted to serve with the army as soon as possible.

At the military school, there were few books available; the teachers had to teach us from memory, and we had to make piles of notes for later reference. Sometime later, we were given books from which we could study for our exams.

During these early weeks in Persia, several officers arrived who knew my father and questioned me, thankfully managing to avoid making it feel like an interrogation.

"So, tell me about yourself," said one of them, "what is your name, where do you come from, and what happened to your father?" I gave him my name and told him where our family had come from but choked up when I tried to tell him what had happened to my father.

"He's dead," was all I managed to get out as I forced that last image of my beloved father back into the deep recesses of my memory. The officer just nodded with evident understanding, explaining to the others who my father was. This was the first time I had experienced the old adage that 'it's not what you know but who you know that counts'. After this I was transferred to an office where my job was to register new recruits and issue their kit.

At first, I was happy with my new position, but after a while of just sitting in an office, I found myself getting jealous of the recruits who were marching and training. I wanted to fight. All through my long walk, my determination to fight for my father had kept me going;

sitting in an office watching others training was not what I had expected. I went and found the officer who had known my father and told him of my determination to fight for my father. He arranged for me to transfer to a unit where I could train and march, but still I wasn't satisfied and went to see him once again.

"Sir, I would like to be in a tank," I said simply, without giving any kind of explanation. If I had been asked, I'm not sure that I could have given one, other than a feeling that in a tank in battle I could survive and continue with this urge to fight.

"Sit tight where you are for now; don't worry about it, I'll make it happen," was the confident reply. His confidence was not misplaced; within six months I had been transferred to a tank unit.

CHAPTER 23

THE MIDDLE EAST (1942-3)

From Persia we were all steadily transported south to Iraq. As we passed through the Persian town of Hamedan, we saw the last of the Russian border guards, with their machine guns, manning the roadblock that marked the southern limit of the territory that they had occupied. From there we continued southwest and camped near a place called Kermanshah, still in Persia, and finally down into Iraq. The journey was long and tedious in the back of those trucks, but I was grateful not to be walking. The further south we travelled the warmer it got and the flatter the landscape. The British had been tasked with defending the Iraqi oil refineries and pipelines, and many of our Polish units were sent there to help with the defence and start their military training.

The training in the desert was very exhausting. The day began at six o'clock in the morning with vigorous exercise, followed by breakfast. Then it was military training until ten o'clock. Because of the heat, which was well over one hundred degrees Fahrenheit in the day, we had a break that lasted until three o'clock in the afternoon. Then in the afternoon we had lectures, and practical instruction in how to service and use artillery guns and so on. After supper and prayers, it was lights out at ten o'clock and we were all ready for a well-earned rest. I relished this new life; I didn't have to think about what I would eat or where it would come from; I didn't have to wonder where I would sleep at night or what I would do the next day, and during this time of training I felt that I had no responsibilities; I could just follow a routine and enjoy learning new skills.

Because of the clear skies, the night temperatures plummeted, especially later in the year. We all lived in tents in the desert like the Bedouins. It reminded me of the weeks I had spent living in tents on my long walk. At times it felt like a strange continuity of my life in exile, that I couldn't expect to live in a permanent dwelling until I went home.

The first morning, as I was about to put on my shoes, one of the other recruits yelled at me in a voice of warning. I leapt in the air not knowing what it was that I had to beware of.

"Hey! You need to check inside before you put your toes in!" he shouted, shaking out his own shoes as he spoke, adding "They're the favourite hiding place for scorpions."

I cautiously picked up my shoes and peered in and then gave them a firm shake just to be sure that there was nothing lurking inside. We had been sleeping under mosquito nets but there still seemed to be millions of flies around that never left us in peace, as well as countless other crawling and flying creatures.

"You'd think after months of being eaten by lice I would be used to creepy crawlies," I said, aware that my lips were curling with disgust at the memory and the thought of having to endure more of these uninvited creatures.

"Just wait till you see a snake," chimed in one of our fellow tent occupants. "The British have been here for long enough to learn all about them," he continued, "I was talking to a chap who told me that there's a whole collection of deadly snakes, like the sand snake. When their soldiers got bitten, they thought it was harmless at first, but then they started to haemorrhage and were dead in two days; and there are the ones that burrow under the sand."

"It's our warm bodies," someone else chipped in, "all these desert creatures are attracted to warmth when it cools down at night."

"What about these scorpions?" I asked, "How deadly are they?"

"I've heard that some are harmless, but others can paralyse you and then you slowly suffocate to death," replied the first fellow, adding, "and don't forget to watch out for the spiky worm-like giant centipede; it may not kill you, but it will cause you severe pain for days if it gets you," he warned ominously. Thankfully, I managed to avoid any snake or scorpion bites, but even with all the precautions and nets, I still ended up having a minor bout of malaria.

In the summer months, the sand in the desert was hot enough to cook eggs on and occasionally we had to endure sandstorms accompanied by electrical storms. I'll never forget my first experience of a sandstorm. Someone was pointing to massive dark clouds in the distance that looked almost like a solid wall, and it was moving towards us at a terrific speed.

"What is that?" he was asking.

"Look out!" called one of the officers, "It's a sandstorm. Take cover and try to cover your nose and mouth."

When it arrived, quite large stones were flung around with the clouds of sand, so that it could be painful if you were struck. The fine sand filled my eyes, hair, and teeth, and even got inside my clothing which was already sticking to me with perspiration. We experienced these sandstorms on several occasions, and at times like this I would compare this hated desert with the beautiful climate and lush green trees of home.

By now I was training in a tank unit. At first, we were using the English Valentine type; the engine was underpowered, and the length of the caterpillar track was not very manoeuvrable. Later, we had the American Sherman tanks. We had to climb up forty-five-degree sloping armour plating on the front, grabbing the main gun barrel to lever ourselves up and into the hatch. The heat inside the tank was indescribable and almost unbearable, especially when we fired our weapons, and the smoke was added to the heat inside the vehicle. Inside were a couple of sprung seats for the driver and co-driver and racks for ammunition; the poor driver had the warmest seat. We used a telescopic sight to find and aim for targets. The Shermans had a crew of five; it was powered by two diesel engines and could go at thirty miles per hour which felt very fast, especially over rough terrain.

As the year rolled on into Autumn, we experienced the rainy season in the desert. At this time, we were camped north of Baghdad near the great river Tigris. Because of the rain, the desert became one great big muddy quagmire. Our trucks just sank into it like quicksand. Sometime before, the British had dug anti-tank ditches for defence. They had left piles of excavated stones and we used these to help stop the trucks from sinking in; it needed at least two layers of these stones to park a truck safely. Autumn and winter rolled into spring, and the desert changed again; the fields were green and full of red tulips. We swam in the river with brown bears and some of the officers went on wild boar hunts on the river islands. Boar meat made a welcome change from the usual Australian mutton.

Our next destination was Palestine. At times, driving across the desert, there were no roads, we just had to keep driving ahead. There were no camp sites on route either, so we had to bivouac on the sand. A makeshift field kitchen was set up when we stopped for the night. Here again we had to watch out for the usual scorpions and snakes, but also different kinds of spiders.

"The tarantulas look scary, but their sting is only like a wasp," one of the men assured me as I checked through my kit and boots for the umpteenth time, shaking out every possible nook and cranny. "But the scariest to look at is the camel spider. They say it can grow up to six inches and runs very fast. I have seen one, it was only small, and it was certainly very ugly, but they're not poisonous to humans", he continued, unaware of my intense dislike of arachnids.

"It's the black widows you have to watch out for," he went on, making my skin begin to crawl. "Their bite can give you cramps and make you sick as a dog for days." As if reading my thoughts, he described what to look for so that I would instantly recognise one if it came into the tent. "They're easy to recognise, obviously they are black, but they have a bright red stripe on the abdomen; I guess it's a kind of warning signal."

We didn't see any scary spiders, but we had quite a few encounters with enormous lizards. On one particular occasion we came across a very big specimen that must have felt threatened by us. It thrashed its tail ferociously like a crocodile and hissed like some giant snake. I'm quite sure the whip from that tail would have been strong enough to break a leg if we had got close enough. Then there were the camels; scruffy looking things with loose bits of old fur hanging off, that roamed at will in the desert and didn't seem to belong to anyone. They spat and made rude noises and fed on huge cacti that had thorns more than an inch long and were hard as nails; they munched away as if it was the soft grass of a Polish pasture.

By the summer, we had travelled through Jordan and were in Palestine, a British mandate at that time. I remember the fruit that we could get in Palestine, fat juicy oranges that seemed to be almost freely available everywhere you went. From the camp, we went on manoeuvres in the mountainous regions mainly in Lebanon and Syria. This was to acclimatise the troops to the kind of terrain we were expected to encounter in Italy. From the higher peaks in the mountains, we could see across to the Mediterranean Sea and the port of Beirut. All the ships in the port had huge anti-aircraft barrage balloons for protection against dive bombers. They looked like a shoal of giant flying silver fish in the air.

For the mountaineering training, we had to climb steep cliffs and follow narrow tracks that were only suitable for goats, and at the same time we had to carry a full pack on our backs forcing us to tip forward to maintain our balance. It was during one of these training exercises that I had my first military injury. We had been walking in single file up a steep and stony track for several hours. I had been challenging myself to keep exactly the same distance from the fellow in front of me, my eyes on his boots that were at my eye level above me and mimicking his steps with a mindless monotony. My thoughts had drifted away for a moment, so that I was suddenly unaware that the rocky path in front of me was loose. My foot slipped on the loose stones, and with the weight of the backpack pulling me down, I found myself sliding at breakneck speed down the hillside, bringing stones and small rocks with me. I had already fallen several dozen feet before I managed to catch hold of a small bush growing in a crevice to break my fall, but as I grabbed it, my whole body swung around, and I was smashed into the cliff face first; in fact, it was nose first because it was my nose that was broken. I suppose I was fortunate that it was only my nose and I lived to tell the tale.

Because so many of us had missed schooling through the war and deportations, it was arranged that during free time from training or combat action, all students and teachers would attend classes and then disperse to their own units. While we were based in Palestine, we also had opportunities to see the sights in the Holy Land. We were able to visit Biblical places like Jerusalem, Bethlehem, Nazareth, and Galilee; some of us even got to swim in the Dead Sea.

Towards the end of the year, the whole division was transferred to Qassasin in Egypt to prepare for the offensive in Italy, using live ammunition. The camp was all tents as elsewhere in the Middle East. There was an outdoor cinema that always seemed to be breaking down and leave parties would go to Cairo, Alexandria, or Ismailia. Once training had finished, we had little to do, so being able to take leave to visit these towns was a welcome distraction. Although when we visited these places we were only allowed to stay in authorised lodgings, we were able to visit the cinemas and clubs that were especially available to military personnel.

In these clubs we met soldiers from other countries, from the British Commonwealth. This was my first real contact with British troops and first sight of Australians, South Africans, and Canadians. Unfortunately, there were occasions when these groups of soldiers aggravated each other, and many fights broke out. Most of the fights were over petty things. One time, when a few of us Poles had gone to the cinema, there was a bit of a scuffle. We were watching a Pathé News reel about Allied troops under General Montgomery in North Africa. Some of the men had put their feet on the backs of the seats in front of them. It was school-boy behaviour, but the pent-up tension about the approaching offensive, and too much free time, led to frayed tempers and the inevitable brawl. Some of the fights were quite serious, usually ending up with all the chairs and tables, and glasses and so on being broken and the army authorities having to pay for the damage.

While we were in Egypt, I felt very fortunate to be able to visit the most fascinating museums. I saw the sphynx and the pyramids at Giza. This historic place was close to the city of Cairo, just a streetcar ride followed by a short walk through a garden. Some of the men had their photographs taken riding on a camel's back in front of the sphynx. After paying for a candle and a tour guide, we could take a tour through a pyramid.

Here I became more closely acquainted with the Arab people. The swarms of children, especially in Cairo, were a constant nuisance and very annoying. They would follow you begging for money, and the shoe-shine boys by the dozen would compete for the chance to clean our shoes, and if they were already clean, they would sneak up behind and smear them with dirt. Sometimes, these boys would even throw liquid polish down your kit if you said that you didn't want your shoes cleaned, and they would cheat you by selling you out-of-date newspapers. There were rumours that some Arabs would cut your throat for a bounty that the Germans were apparently offering for your pay book.

At that time, Egypt nevertheless seemed to be a prosperous country; the cities were a wonderful sight to my eyes starved for so long from seeing beautiful shops. The magnificent jewellery and the shop windows containing bars of gold for sale were a real shock to me. For the first time since leaving home I had money to spend and shops to spend it in. I bought myself a beautiful pair of leather shoes and a few souvenirs. Many of the older men invested their army pay in gold coins that they considered a good investment.

During this time, I was recruited into the military police and was sent for training in a Staff school to acquaint myself with the paperwork. There was a great deal to learn of the legal requirements of the job. I found all this very time-consuming work; the police records had to be precisely kept, as the records would follow the troops around. The records also had to be unbiased and strictly accurate. It wasn't very inspiring work, and I didn't feel that it was a role in which I would still feel that I was fighting for my country and my father. When the studies reached the stage that we covered the penalties that would have to be paid for by soldiers committing a crime, including the death sentence by firing squad for desertion, I decided that I could not possibly continue with this training, and I applied to go back into tanks.

Towards the end of the year, we boarded ships destined for Italy. At the port in Alexandria, the duty Destroyer fired depth charges every hour to deter enemy frogmen from planting limpet mines on the sides of the ships, so we didn't get much sleep. We embarked for the invasion of Italy as part of the first prong of the offensive the next morning.

CHAPTER 24

ITALY (1944)

There was standing room only on the troop ship as our convoy headed out into the Mediterranean Sea, bound for the Italian coast. Calm seas would have made this more tolerable, but it was a rough crossing in more ways than one. Because of the overcrowding, we felt like sitting ducks when the Luftwaffe appeared, screaming across the sky, strafing our boats with machine-gun fire, and dropping bombs. There was nothing we could do as the planes circled around us. The dive bombers hit at least one of our boats. The black smoke from the exploding ship turned day into night for hours. We were unable to pick up many survivors. When we finally landed in Italy, teaming up with the British Eighth Army that had been in action in Sicily, we were joined for the first time by American troops.

Although the Italian Army had capitulated by this stage, and the local population welcomed us in, the German defences were well established, and they had used their time in Italy to learn the lie of the land and plan effective strategic defences using the natural defences of the mountainous landscape. Our Allied Forces were tasked with pushing the German line north with the aim of taking Rome and then the rest of Italy, our ultimate objective being to push the Germans completely out of Italy.

My impression of Italy was of a population who were thin, pale, and war-weary; there was evidence of real poverty and devastation, and poorly clad hungry children would come up to us begging for anything that might be on offer. After the heat of the Middle East, it was a shock to be back in the wet and cold and to have to contend with rivers of mud. Further north the rain turned to snow and with strong winds blowing there were times when we encountered deep drifts sometimes as much as three or four metres deep. Bridges and roads had been damaged or destroyed, and many of the villages that we passed through had bombed out houses.

After landing at Taranto, I was transferred back to the special unit keeping personnel records in preparation for the heavy casualties that were expected. Whenever there was a shortage of troops due to injuries or deaths, I was transferred, along with other administrative staff, into a fighting unit. I happily volunteered to go behind enemy lines to unpick the mines from underneath bridges. Assigned to a tank unit, my Italian campaign began with me receiving minor shrapnel injuries in tank skirmishes.

Inside a tank it was almost impossible to sleep, as each member of the crew had to be constantly on the alert. The pressure was intense, and sometimes we couldn't sleep properly for three nights in a row. The sound of the smack of bullets, shrapnel, and debris hitting the armour outside would keep us on tenterhooks as it threatened something large and more penetrating. In the early months of the campaign, the air inside the cramped conditions was not only foul but was icy cold in the early mornings or when the engine had been stopped for a while. It was freezing in the Apennine winter, and it was boiling in the summer months. When we were in action, firing high-explosive shells, the turret became a hell of cordite fumes and hot brass shell casings.

But there were lulls between battles when we did our best to enjoy ourselves. On one occasion, we were driving through a small town that had been heavily bombarded. One of our men spotted a wine store where the front window had been blown out and bottles of wine stood undamaged on the shelves of the shop.

"Stop the tank!" he shouted, "Free wine!"

The tank came to a halt, and we all scrabbled to look in the direction he was pointing.

"The Americans take the wine on board; they do it all the time, I've seen it," someone reminded us. "They store it on the ammunition racks."

"I've heard that some of them keep chickens to lay eggs in their tanks," laughed someone else.

"What about the ammunition?" I asked doubtfully, ignoring the talk about chickens, and very aware of how much of a breach of discipline this would be, and what the repercussions might be if we were caught.

"If we only throw out half the ammunition and replace it with the wine, then we will still have some ammo to fire, and maybe the tank commander won't notice that we're not firing at full capacity," was someone else's hesitant suggestion. In the end we took the risk, but only once, and counted ourselves very fortunate not to have been discovered.

Our next wine incident was very different. Our tank crew, along with two others, was pushing through against a German position. We had moved beyond the enemy's line and unbeknown to us, and without any warning, the Germans had advanced around us so that we were effectively cut off behind enemy lines.

"There's no time to prepare ourselves for a fight," I yelled, having summed up the situation. "There are not enough of us, and I for one don't intend to be taken prisoner; we need to get out and under cover now!"

There were only fourteen of us and we weren't able to take much equipment with us as we hid amongst the rubble of the demolished buildings.

"How far away do you think our troops are?" asked one of the men, probably wondering if we could make a quick run for it.

"They can't be far away," I said, "but we would have no chance of getting through. Our best chance is to avoid being detected and hope our troops retake the area soon."

We had no idea how long that might take, or even if it would happen at all; our biggest problem was going to be sustenance. We split up into small reconnaissance groups to look for possible sources of food and drink. The Germans already seemed to have stripped the area of most of its food supplies. Our group commandeered a few chickens and eggs from a local farmer who had probably been saving them for his family. We left him a note telling him to claim a repayment from the British Army when they arrived.

"We can't stay hidden in all this rubble; we'll look for some farm buildings that have dry cellars where we can hide. I think we should stay in our small units," I suggested.

Under cover of dark, we made our way to some farm outbuildings and what looked like an abandoned farmhouse and checked out the cellars. As we started to go down some stone steps on the outside of the building that stood on a slope, we could hear someone softly humming to themselves. We stopped in our tracks, slowed our breathing to soundless mode, and listened intently. Periodically, the humming broke into singing that we could recognise as Italian. Friend or foe was the question in all our minds. A short, burly figure came into view, silhouetted against the moonlight behind him. He looked like a local man who was probably the owner of the farm of which we were at that moment lurking in the shadows. None of us knew much Italian, so I took a risk and addressed him in German. The poor fellow nearly died of fright, holding his hands up and pleading with me not to shoot. I stepped out of the shadows so that he could see me and pointed to the insignias on my uniform.

"Polish," I told him in German. "We are not Germans; we are Polish and mean you no harm." He slowly lowered his arms and shrugged his shoulders.

"Polish?" he echoed.

I wasn't sure if he didn't know who we were or if he didn't know what Polish meant.

"Friends," I said, hoping that this would be more successful. It was, and to show that he was happy to be friends he told us that we were welcome to stay anywhere on his farm that we thought might be safe.

"Do you have food and water that you could share with us?" I asked hopefully. "We escaped from the Germans without any supplies, and I don't know how long we will need to stay hidden," I explained unnecessarily. He nodded his understanding, gave a beaming smile, and confirmed that he understood, saying in a rich, deep voice,

"Food. Food and drink for the men," before retracing his steps with a mock tiptoe that he thought hilariously funny and then hushing himself and whispering something conspiratorially, and to me incomprehensible, in Italian.

We had been in hiding for a few days when one night our friendly farmer decided to share some of his best wine. He waddled down the stone steps into the basement, feeling his way cautiously down, and sliding his back against the wall for stability, as he carefully cradled a container in both arms. Once safely at the bottom, he took a large spoon out of his pocket and poured out a spoonful of jelly-like substance.

"Wine," he said with evident pride, "The best. From my family." He offered the spoon to the soldier nearest him.

"I'm not sure," said the intended recipient, looking dubiously at the spoon, "it looks suspicious to me."

"Yes, yes. Try it," encouraged the farmer, "It is for special guests. It is very good," he said trying to reassure us. He was very persuasive, and in the end we all had a few spoonfuls. It had a very strong, wonderful fruity flavour, and although it was dry there was no acidity or bitterness. But after about ten minutes or so we began to feel rather strange. Wondering if I needed some fresh air, I tried to stand up and to my horror found that my legs had turned to jelly. The others then tried to stand up and found that they too had no strength in their legs.

"That treacherous old farmer," said one of the men, expressing all our thoughts, "He must be in league with the Germans. He must have been planning how to disarm us all the time he was pretending to make friends."

"Maybe he has just poisoned us," said one of the others angrily. I was more angry than afraid and called the farmer down to the cellar, ordering him to explain what his purpose was. The farmer came nervously back down the steps and shrank back in terror when he saw that several of us had our revolvers pointing straight at him. He slowly raised his arms, trembling all over with fear. His throat must have been dry because his voice had lost its musical tone and came out in a husky rasp.

"What have I done? What are you going to do to me?" he rasped out in evident surprise at the turn of events.

"You have poisoned us. We will kill you before we die," I told him angrily. The farmer lowered his arms and burst into peals of laughter, his round figure heaving with each guffaw.

"It is very old wine," he said between deep breaths, "about two hundred years. It is from a special family recipe. There is hardly any left; I give it only to special visitors. You will not die," he told us before breaking out into more full-bellied laughter.

"Don't believe him," said one of our men, "keep him covered."

"If we start to die, then the last one alive must shoot the farmer," said another, and we all agreed. The poor farmer was forced to sit there on the step with a gun pointed at him for a couple of hours until we all regained the use of our legs.

"Never. Never again will I give away my best wine. I sacrificed my best wine for you thinking you were friends and liberators, but you did not appreciate it. You threatened my life," he said indignantly when we finally let him go.

After that we decided to move from his farmhouse, and whilst searching for food, we found an empty house that seemed to have been abandoned in a hurry. The house was located further up in the valley on a steep incline that was difficult to negotiate when we were restricted to moving only under cover of night. We made a thorough investigation, and once we were convinced that there were no Germans about, we installed ourselves in the attic of the farmhouse.

"We need to make look-out holes on all sides," I said, "and then we need to organise some traps downstairs to warn us if anyone comes into the building." I volunteered to lay the traps having had a great deal of practice in my Scouting days. They were just simple things like leaning objects against the inside of cupboard doors so that they would fall if someone pulled the door open and dropping things that would crunch unseen underfoot. We searched through the house for any remaining food and took it up into the attic along with jugs and cups of water so that we wouldn't need to leave the attic at least until our supplies ran out.

At the back of the farmhouse, a forest ran steeply up behind, and to the front the ground fell away into the valley. It was a good defensive position, and we were able to relax for a while. Having organised a look-out rota, I let myself drift off to sleep the first night, looking forward to some well-earned rest.

In the early hours of dawn, I awoke in a cold sweat as I emerged from a nightmare in which wolves chased me through deep snow. My feet kept sinking down so far that I couldn't pull them up; I couldn't get away and the wolves were almost upon me. The sound of the wolves howling was so loud and real that it stayed with me as I woke up. It was several moments before I realised that I was in fact awake and it must be real wolves that I could hear outside the farmhouse. I silently worked my way past the sleeping men and found a look-out hole. Sure enough, just at the line of the first trees rising behind the house, I could see a handful of wolves lurking in the shadows. Thankfully, this was the only time I saw or heard wolves in the Apennine Mountains.

The following night we were disturbed by a very different visitation. It was during my watch, and I distinctly heard the sound of soft footsteps, and a slight crunch, on the stone floor below us. Putting my hand gently over the mouth of those sleeping, I woke each of the sleeping men, indicating that they must be silent and keep absolutely still. We sat listening, hardly daring to breathe. I indicated with hand signs that the chap nearest the ladder to the attic should try to get a look at who, or what, we could hear. He took his boots off and was just about to begin to lower himself onto the first rung when he froze, and we all heard the subdued whisper of voices. We waited, hearts thudding in our chest, each one of us unconsciously planning what to do if or when we had to move into action. I indicated to the chap on the ladder to count how many people had entered the building by counting on my fingers. He lowered himself very slowly, the muscles in his arms trembling with the effort.

It seemed an age before he reappeared and silently indicated that there were six men. He carefully hauled himself back up into the attic, tiptoed to the furthest wall and then spoke as quietly as he could.

"Men, six I think," He said warningly, "they searched the building, but I don't think they were looking for anyone, just looking for somewhere to sleep like us. They have gone into the kitchen."

"We'll give them a couple of hours to settle down, then we can go down and see who they are and exactly how many of them," I said in equally hushed tones.

When all was quiet, weapons in hand, we stealthily crept down from the attic and made our way towards the kitchen. To our horror, we discovered that they were German soldiers. They must have been absolutely exhausted because they slept so heavily that they did not hear us as we stood looking down at them. We could see that one of them was a sergeant, another a member of the medical corps, and the rest were privates. I indicated to a couple of our men to check outside to see if there were anymore, and if the coast was clear, while we kept them covered. It was just six of them against all of us; they had no chance. I woke them up, speaking in crisp German,

“Wake up! Hands up! We have you covered.”

In a matter of seconds, they were disarmed and sat up disbelievingly; they had clearly thought themselves alone in the house. I had spoken to them in German and so they showed no signs of fear.

“Whose idea of a joke is this?” asked the sergeant with evident irritation.

“This is no joke,” I told him, “We are Polish, and you are now our prisoners.”

“Polish? You speak German,” said the medic still thinking this was some kind of joke being played on them.

“Yes, I speak Russian too. We are from Polish Second Corps, part of the British Eighth Army, and we have captured you,” I assured him.

They finally grasped the reality of their position and began to show signs of fear. We found out that the medic had come from an area near Gdansk, the so-called Polish Corridor, and he spoke the local dialect Kashubisz, but we were able to converse in Polish and assured him that we weren't going to shoot them. We would hand them over to the British when they arrived. We had no way of knowing if the British Army would be arriving or how long it might be if they did, but this assurance seemed to calm our prisoners. They accepted the situation and even shared their rations with us which cheered us up no end.

There was no point killing the Germans in cold blood. They were very nice chaps and caused us no harm at all, but now we had to keep ourselves hidden, and keep them prisoner, and all the while we were still behind enemy lines. Safe inside the farmhouse, we all became very friendly.

"I'll be glad when this war is over," said the medic, "so that I can return to my family." We were all so much in accord with this statement that there was nothing to be said; nothing to add.

One of the Germans, thinking about his own family, fished out a photograph of his wife and children.

"This is my wife and children," he said, proudly showing the photograph around. "I had hoped to be sent home and see them when I was badly wounded on the Eastern Front, but they put me in a field hospital and then I was sent here to Italy," he told us, forgetting that we were barely acquainted and 'the enemy'. However, this happy time of respite was short lived.

Later that same day, just as I had begun wondering what we would do for supplies if our situation remained the same for much longer, we heard the distant sound of gunfire. We all stopped talking and listened intently. The sound was definitely getting closer, and after a few minutes, shells began landing and exploding all around the farmhouse. Not knowing which troops were coming our way, we Poles took up defensive positions and prepared ourselves for a fight, while the Germans pleaded with us to hand them over to the British Army so that they could be in the relative safety of a prisoner of war camp.

Fortunately for us, the Allied troops were pushing the German line back, driving them north away from us. When our troops finally reached our hiding place, we handed our German prisoners over to the Military Police and they were gratefully taken to a place of safety. We then had to return to our unit, who had already posted us as 'Missing behind enemy lines'. We had managed to evade capture for ten days.

In another memorable experience, when we were confronting the Germans, we had found ourselves in a position where we were heavily outnumbered. By this time in the Italian campaign, the Allies had superiority in the skies, with air force bases located on the south-eastern coast of Italy. We knew that some of our Allied positions had requested close air support during battles; the United States Air Force had harassed German troop movements and supressed their artillery fire. We knew that the weather often kept the aircraft grounded because of poor visibility, but on this occasion, there were perfect weather conditions, and the target was clearly visible. Our commanding officer radioed for air support.

When the planes came over, to our dismay, instead of bombing and strafing the German positions, they bombed us instead. They inflicted heavy casualties on our already weak position. Having witnessed the inaccuracy of the Allied Air Force bombing, we were reluctant to call for close air support in the future. Of course, the front line could change very quickly, sometimes making it difficult to pinpoint the enemy area, meaning that mistakes were made with devastating effect, but such are the fortunes of war.

CHAPTER 25

MONTE CASSINO (1944)

In April, we began moving northwest towards the German defensive line that stretched right across Italy from coast to coast, spanning the Apennine Mountain range that ran like a central spine down the Italian boot. We were headed for the section known as the Gustav Line. Preparations for the attack were being made in absolute secrecy. To avoid being spotted by German planes, we drove in trucks at night without lights, following the truck in front of us. The terrain was mountainous with winding roads and treacherously steep drops, such a contrast with the flat desert landscape where we had recently spent so much time. On the long trip we couldn't risk cooking and had to live mostly on dry food.

We arrived near the foothills of Monte Cassino towards the end of the month. As soon as we approached the Sangro River, close to Venafro, about ten miles from the font line, we came under fire by German artillery. We had reached the valley in which the town of Cassino had once nestled peacefully at the foot of the mountains and was now a heap of rubble. At first, we camped in one of the many olive groves several kilometres from the town. We pitched our tiny, cramped kennel-like tents in the rain and were grateful that they didn't leak. From the edge of our campsite, we could look across the wide flat-bottomed valley with its straight Roman roads to the smoking ruins of the monastery high on its awesome perch. At the other end of the valley were steep mountains. I remember the view across the wide valley below the monastery that was covered with beautiful flowers in the distance, bright red poppies. As we drew closer to the battle zone, the red delicate flowers that fluttered in the breeze seemed in stark contrast with the death and destruction that littered the roads and riverbanks around us.

The monastery, that by this time had become infamous, sat perched high up on the mountain side above the small town of Cassino. It had stood on this lofty point over-looking the valley since the sixth century. The German defensive line straddled the monastery, making it an inevitable target in spite of its antiquity and cultural and religious importance. We knew that it had already been under siege for many months. By the time we arrived on the scene, there was nothing but a ruin to be seen of the once beautiful and historic building. We were told that there had already been three unsuccessful campaigns against this stronghold of German paratroopers by the Americans, and the British, Canadian, Indian, and New Zealand armies. Our commanding officer informed us that the German elite troops had been given the task of halting the Allied invasion on the road to Rome. After many months of bloodshed and hardship, the Army Chiefs of Staff had decided that we, the Polish Second Corps, under the leadership of General Anders, would attempt another assault.

"What makes them think that we can succeed when all these others have failed?" asked one of the men in my unit.

"Our job is to isolate the German forces from their lines of supply and reserves. We will be crossing the Rapido River and making an assault on Monte Cassino by sneaking around the back of the monastery. This should allow the British, the Eighth Army, to advance along the Liri Valley," was the prosaic answer he received.

"You mean they looked at their divisions and asked themselves, 'Who are the sneakiest?' and decided it was the Poles," said the soldier with a sour laugh.

The monastery, on its magnificent perch, looked down on the town of Cassino, and more importantly, on the main highway, Route 6, to Rome. The Allied forces could not risk advancing northwards along Route 6, or over the flat river plain, towards Rome while the Germans could fire with ease on them from the monastery and the high ground surrounding it. Looking up at the ruin, a cadet officer, echoing my own thoughts, said,

"Even though it's a ruin, it still looks to me like an enemy barracks teeming with Germans. I bet the enemy are watching us from every one of those strange little windows in that wall that is somehow still standing."

As we moved nearer to our positions, the landscape changed. It had been pulverised by the earlier battles. Even from a distance, we could see the fallen bodies scattered on the mountain slopes below the monastery. There were only tree stumps with grotesque bare limbs, not one tree had any of its fresh green Spring leaves. There was no grass where endless trucks and tanks had driven over the ground and turned everything to mud and bare rock; a pall of thick grey dust lay over everything. Decomposing bodies of men and animals, some covered in lime, lay stinking in the mud. The stench was suffocating, and there were fat, engorged flies everywhere. Some of the men used bandages to make a facemask, putting poppy petals in between the layers to try to disguise the overpowering odour. To me that seemed like too much effort, and I doubted that it would have much effect. But I did collect handfuls of petals and crush them to hold against my nose for some brief respite for my senses. Moving as a column, we followed the white tape marking our safe passage past the leafless and mangled trees, past ruined farmhouses, enormous shell holes filled with water and edged with mud, and through the minefields.

The constant enemy surveillance forced us to move only at night and kept us pinned down during the day. The enemy had an excellent view into the valley and the slope of the hills. In the valley, where there used to be a bustling community, everything looked dead. The abandoned white, square stone houses, with windows blown out, were devoid of life. The debris of discarded equipment from former battles littered the roads. If we were travelling with trucks when the nights were especially dark, with no moonlight, one of us had to walk in front of the truck with a white cloth laid across their shoulder to show the way. Artillery guns and ammunition were moved into their positions on the mountains and in the valleys under cover of night. Our trucks were covered in branches and brushwood to give us some camouflage. Where trucks couldn't go any further, ammunition had to be pulled up the mountainsides with ropes from the place where the trucks had to stop.

Our entire division was moved slowly and stealthily in small units to maintain the secrecy, and once in position, we were ordered not to carry out reconnaissance missions.

"There is too great a risk of prisoners being taken, and of course this could lead to the failure of the operation," our commanding officer told us. The implications were obvious to us. Later, when we were nearer our final positions, we were told to deliver anything that could identify us to headquarters.

"All personal papers, letters and so on that can identify you by name or regiment must be collected up and handed to the regimental office," we were warned. I didn't have any letters to worry about, but some of the fellows who had sweethearts were reluctant to hand over their precious letters.

"When can we get them back? I haven't memorised my latest letter yet," asked one fellow who looked downright miserable about having to give them up.

"Why do you memorise your letters?" I asked him with genuine interest.

"It calms my nerves when I recite them to myself," he replied bashfully, "I guess it's a distraction from all of this," he added with a sweeping movement of his arm indicating the entire cursed valley. The only things we were allowed to retain were the dog tags and equipment – one blanket, mess kit, rifle, and ammunition.

Because of the need for silence, in the continuing optimism for a surprise attack, we were given sneakers, canvas shoes, or rubber boots for our stealthy march into the hills. Talking was absolutely forbidden. For us, tanks were abandoned, and we ascended the mountain on foot. At the foot of the hills, we crossed the fast flowing, aptly named, Rapido River via a wooden bridge. We waited for convoy mules to come down a narrow footpath that was only wide enough for one person or mule. Climbing the hills outside the footpath was impossible because of land mines. We climbed the narrow path, shells exploding in the spot we had just left, walking in complete silence. We walked with our heads down or blackened. The Germans were positioned in such a way that they dominated the entire valley; we were fired on while we were still down on the lowest slopes.

We followed the narrow path marked by the white tape that fluttered between the thin posts like the tape at the scene of a crime. Higher in the mountains we were shown where our soldiers were positioned, hidden in different gullies. There were so many soldiers spread over this mountainous region that it took us several nights to locate them all and memorise their positions and then report this information back to our superior officers.

In these mountains, where jeeps couldn't go, mules took over, led by volunteers including Cypriots and Palestinians. The muleteers had to follow their white-taped paths through muddy minefields and rocky mountain trails sometimes for twelve-hour return journeys. Where the tracks petered out, the mules had to be left behind and the men had to carry the heavy loads on their backs, securely fastened to avoid overbalancing into the valley below. Scrabbling up the steep hillside, we often had to use our hands to get a grip.

"You need to stow your rifle somewhere," I told one fellow who stood looking up at the rocks evidently trying to decide how to get up there without letting go of his weapon; his white knuckles showing how fiercely he was gripping his gun. He gave me a blank look.

"If you fall here, you've got no chance," I said bluntly, "so stow your rifle and use your hands."

We were all heavily loaded down with equipment and supplies; the mules carried the ammunition in heavy steel boxes and were led by all sorts of people from different nationalities, including the local Italians. We scrambled up the hillside in single file and I was amazed at how much easier the mules seemed to find the climb than us humans, even though they were so heavily laden. Periodically we would have to stop and try to make way for a mule train coming down. Often, they were transporting the wounded. The narrow mountain path was littered with boulders, and frequently rocks and other debris came tumbling down. If we were caught by enemy fire, we took what cover we could, but the animals often broke loose and went hurtling down the precipitous hill sides, or they would be hit and then some poor fellow would have to try to carry the heavy load themselves.

Whenever we were on the move, we had to move as stealthily as possible, sometimes hardly daring to breathe in case we made our presence known to an enemy patrol. Each time a loose rock was dislodged and fell noisily, we froze in our tracks as the Germans, or our own patrols, fired flares into the sky illuminating the mountainside. We would hug the ground there until word was passed back that it was safe to continue.

Preparations for the attack continued to be made in total secrecy. Daytime movement was strictly controlled, noise was supressed, and normal routines had to continue to give the impression that no attack was imminent.

As April turned into May, the heat began to be a problem, especially with supplies of water. For food we were given biscuits, beef, and bacon. A few of the men complained that it was barely edible, but those of us who had gone through starvation in Siberia made the most of it. I knew how little I could survive on and so long as I had some food, I knew I would have the strength to fight on. But water was rationed and became a very precious commodity.

Sheltering in any available gullies, we watched as volunteer porters acted as stretcher bearers bringing the wounded down from the mountain ledges. If there was room, there would be four men carrying the stretcher, but often it was only wide enough for two and we could hear the wounded soldier groan as the stretcher bearers slipped and stumbled over the rocks on their descent. Sometimes it would be only one brave fellow having to carry his burden across his shoulder like a fireman because it was just too steep for a stretcher. These men may not have been fighting but their courage was as heroic as any soldier; they must have saved countless lives. Mules were also used to bring the wounded down off the mountainside. For those who were able to sit up, there were basket-like seats attached either side of the mules like paniers, and for those more seriously wounded there were large oval-shaped basket paniers that made the mules look very unstable.

Gradually we made our preparations. The rocky terrain meant that we could only dig slit trenches to protect ourselves from shrapnel and flying splintered rock. Most casualties on this terrain were caused by mortar rounds or artillery, the injuries made worse by the hard rocky ground where even small fragments of rock could rip and tear with deadly effect. We climbed to the designated position at night and spent our days in trenches. It was necessary to find some angle or crevice under the rock, dig a hole, and then using special bags put stones into them to create a hiding place. I took out and looked over the small steel entrenching tool with which we had been issued for this purpose.

"This thing isn't much good," I complained with frustration as the tool made hardly any impression on the stony ground. "We can't dig properly here; it's going to be too shallow to give any protection." Looking around us we could see that other fellows had used sandbags or any other kind of sack and filled them with any old rubble and stones to build a kind of shelter. One of the men in our unit began doing the same, filling a bag with whatever heavy objects he could scoop up.

"If we stay here long enough, we can build a dry-wall fortress. Of course, it won't protect us from shells and mortars if we get a direct hit but at least it should protect us from shrapnel and flying shards of rock," said the soldier who seemed to be enjoying having some kind of practical occupation as he carefully measured rocks and stones fitting them together to make his wall.

A smoke screen filled the entire valley so that we couldn't be seen, but neither could we see the German positions. They sat quietly, sometimes firing mortars at night, but their artillery was silent. Every now and again someone would try to take aim and then we would hear rapid machine-gun fire and in between complete silence. Our artillery had to be moved as far forward as possible in the valley. The artillery, just as everything else, could only be moved at night and had to be well camouflaged and remain silent. We kept the smoke screen going the whole time. The deep sinking mud of the river valley prevented even four-wheeled drive trucks from getting close to the positions which meant columns of men and mules silently picking their way through at night without light, carrying loads forward.

This new nocturnal life was exhausting, but at times was strangely exhilarating. Pinned down in our flimsy shelters during the day, we tried to catch up on sleep, but for me it was mostly an uneasy sleep as I tried to keep part of my mind awake to listen out for sounds of threatened danger. It was a relief to see a spotter plane on fine days because it stopped all the mortars and guns firing at us. If they had kept firing, the spotter plane would have been able to locate their position. It was a little old biplane that used to fly high overhead and we would get a short quiet period for about twenty minutes.

I have never smoked, but many of our chaps had taken up the habit and I could see that it helped calm their nerves. But each time someone lit up a cigarette they took a great risk.

“I guess you have heard what happened to the Americans?” I asked one chap. We had heard stories about the Americans who had been there before us and how they had been careless when they smoked their cigarettes. The German snipers plucked them off one by one.

“Perhaps one clean shot to the head would be a good way to go,” he grimaced, but turned away to hide the glow all the same.

The Polish Second Corp had been tasked with the attack and capture of the area of the monastery hill from the north and northeast. Our division, the Third Carpathian, were to move along a ridge of peaks and destroy the German defences overlooking the monastery, while the other division advanced a long a second ridge. The German positions on these ridges that ran in circles were like the seats in the top row of an amphitheatre from which every scrap of ground could be seen with no possibility of an attacker approaching unseen. This really was a theatre of war, and we were to be the gladiators, thrown together by the will of the evil empire builders.

On May eleventh, the First Brigade launched our first attack. On the day, the weather was overcast, and it rained. As evening fell, I wondered if we had been successful in all our attempts at secrecy or if the Germans knew exactly what was about to occur and were fully prepared. The stillness of the night was interrupted occasionally by bursts of machine gun fire from both sides. The silence in between was uncanny.

Artillery units had been set up on every available space. At 11 o'clock, all hell broke loose from the Allied guns all along the valley. The non-stop firing above our heads lasted for hours creating a deafening, overwhelming continuous roar. It was pandemonium. The thunder from the guns even caused the ground to move. All the artillery of the American 5th and the British 8th armies, including the artillery of our 2nd Corps were unleashed against the enemy positions. The barrage of artillery shells lit the sky as brightly as daylight; the valley was suddenly filled with light. Tracers streaked across a multicoloured sky. I remember thinking the light was bright enough to read a newspaper by. A sea of fire changed night into day like a firework spectacle.

The air overhead was full of thousands of shells whining and screeching. The noise reduced us to sign language. We learned afterwards that the artillery barrage was so intense that the ears, noses, and eyes of the artillery crews were bleeding. The barrel of the canons became so hot that they periodically had to stop firing and cover them with wet sheets to cool down. Some barrels became so hot that they separated from the canons; they simply fell off. The crews were unable to speak or hear properly for three days after. We were all so exhausted that at one point a blast threw one of the men who was sleeping from his place, and he did not even wake up. Stones were flying from all sides. At one point I had an overwhelming desire to get out into an open field away from any enclosure; the noise seemed to close in so that somehow, I felt trapped in a cage of almost tangible noise.

There was nothing to see on the ground because of the smoke from the explosions. Soon even the shell bursts could no longer be seen, as they were smothered by the smoke. Allied bombers circled over the enemy positions, attacking targets guided in by our troops. From above, with all the smoke, I doubt they could see much. The German counterattack was ferocious, and our troops were eventually forced to retreat.

When the dust settled, we could see in the valley twisted human shapes and shattered bodies. These latest victims lay with those of various nations from earlier battles, some of which had been there since January. The place came alive with rats, big, bloated creatures that scurried about without retribution while we slept. The sickly-sweet smell of rotting flesh of both man and beast grew nauseating in the May heat and we couldn't escape it.

After our first attack, the Germans knew that the Polish army had taken over the offensive positions. Day and night we were assailed by a barrage of propaganda through loudspeakers and radio broadcasts. They used the voice of a woman called Wanda who spoke in Polish, trying to demoralise us. She told us that we would be better off joining the German army as the British would not help us. She spoke in a sugary voice, telling us in Polish,

"Your land has been delivered to Stalin's hands by Churchill. You have no place to return to when the war is done. What are you poor boys doing fighting in Italy? The Bolsheviks are entering your homeland and burning your houses and raping your women. It's easy for you to get close to your loved ones. All you need do is cross over the front line and say, 'I want to go home'."

We answered Wanda with bursts of machine gun fire and mortars. They even dropped leaflets over our positions printed in Polish, telling us to give up, pick up a leaflet, join them, and they promised to repatriate us to Poland to join our families and live in peace in our own country. This propaganda enraged us all the more, so that we were fighting mad.

We knew that the Germans had a network of strong well-concealed bunkers, so they were able to fire on our positions from the monastery and other high ground. Most of our units were under constant mortar and small arms fire, and our rear positions were exposed to artillery fire. Constant barrage from our artillery kept German units underground. Our artillery continued to bombard key sections of the German positions while our units regrouped, and air support of fighter bombers continued to target concealed German artillery in the mountains. One of the scariest of the German weapons was nicknamed Moaning Minnie by the British; it was very accurate. Six rockets would be launched at the same time giving off a high-pitched scream. The moaning sound got louder as it approached and then changed to a deafening roar; the explosions rocked the ground. At night we could more easily locate a target because the flashes from the gun bursts would give away its position. During the day it became difficult to work out the range and direction because of the echo effect in the mountains that made the sound come at you in all directions.

Some of the men who hadn't yet been in action were beginning to suffer from the stress of inaction. Some of them started to complain of headaches, diarrhoea, dizziness, and shooting pains in the chest. They huffed and puffed but felt that they couldn't catch their breath. For days we lived in a shifting murk of drifting smoke, heavy with the pestilential reek of death. The ground still periodically trembled under the artillery barrage, but weirdly at night, when the guns stopped firing, we could occasionally hear nightingales singing.

During these days, we never seemed to have any rest or sleep, or opportunity to eat even when provisions managed to get through. But the worst, during this period of waiting, was the sight of the decomposing bodies that no one could collect because there was never any cease fire.

There were night patrols when we would creep over towards the German line and, more often than not, they would creep over towards our line, sometimes at the same time so that we might meet in the middle. Not daring to speak, we would use sign language to indicate where we thought an enemy patrol might be. We would peer out into the darkness, hoping to avoid craters in the total dark. We would fire at each other and throw grenades. If it was a full moon, we wouldn't go. When out on these night patrols we had to divest ourselves of anything that could identify us and wore our canvas sneakers instead of boots. One time, we got so close to a German patrol that I could hear their conversation. I calmly indicated that our patrol should immediately halt and maintain absolute silence. I dared not engage in combat at this proximity for fear of being shot at by both sides, by the Germans and our own troops. I indicated that the patrol should slowly squat down so that if we accidently betrayed ourselves by making even the smallest sound, they would shoot over our heads. The moment passed and we returned unscathed.

On May seventeenth, we launched the second attack, with our Second Brigade, and concentrated our artillery support on one main target, with a rolling barrage to cover the advancing infantry. By this time, after sending out numerous patrols, we had a better idea of the terrain and the location of the German positions. The battle commenced with several hours of heavy artillery fire as we lay waiting. It was absolutely deafening, and no one could hear any conversation or any other sounds. The moment the guns ceased we commenced our attack.

When the second attack began, many of our troops were already drained. We had first to climb to the summit, carrying as many grenades as we could, together with machine guns and flame-throwing equipment. It was very difficult to flush out the Germans as they were in deep underground bunkers and had abandoned the monastery buildings, or what was left of them. Some of the weariest men were not able to keep pace with the rest of us. I became aware that we were no longer in any proper formation; I couldn't tell exactly where all my platoon was. We were left to our own initiative to engage with the enemy, often in hand-to-hand combat. In the confusion German positions seemed mixed with ours. We hurled our hand grenades in the direction we presumed the enemy to be, whilst from the neighbouring heights we were caught in a deadly crossfire of heavy machine guns.

To reach the starting point, we had climbed in the dark for about twenty kilometres in muddy mountainous terrain. Now we were slowed by a terrain that was covered with a deadly combination of thorn bush, barbed wire, and anti-personnel mines scattered liberally about. As we approached our target point, expecting the Germans to have already been driven back, we could see that they were still there, and we were suddenly fired on from the rear. We could see the Germans just a stone's throw away, but we dared not fire on them because once having given away our location we would have received the full brunt of their artillery. Tanks that had been destroyed in earlier battles had been turned into small pill boxes by the Germans.

As we ascended the steep hillside, we were targeted by mortars. We hit the deck clinging to the ground as they rained down around us. Then there was a noise like thunder. It was right on my head. There was a high-pitched whistle in my ears, and I blacked out.

I learned later that our units attacked with great fury in revenge for the destruction of our homeland. After many hours struggling to the summit, our troops drove out the remaining Germans, and the Polish flag was hoisted on the ruins of the monastery. We lost thousands of lives in this battle, but at last the Germans were dislodged and the road to Rome was open. A few German prisoners were taken, and I heard that one of them later remarked that they were absolutely stunned by the ferocity and bravery of the units who took them. They thought we were invincible.

From my unit of a hundred and twenty men, only seventeen survived. I was very lucky to survive the battle but had been seriously wounded in the head by a mortar shell that came straight down from above without warning, and I was transferred by plane to a Polish military hospital.

CHAPTER 26

THE LONG ROAD TO RECOVERY (1944)

I slowly opened my eyes; there was dazzling bright whiteness around me. From somewhere nearby came a subdued hum of what sounded like distant conversation. White figures seemed to be drifting around me. Questions chased through my mind. Was I dead? If I was looking around, I must be moving my eyes; would that happen if I was dead? I tried to move but nothing happened. I must have died, but surely the next life wouldn't smell of antiseptic. No, it must be a dream. I tried to think, but my thoughts floated away before I could catch hold of them. Dead or dreaming. It's not real, was the only thought that kept still long enough to hang on to in the empty space of my mind. Then the brightness faded, everything became dark, and I sank back into a blanket of nothingness.

Time must have passed; my eyes opened once again onto a wall of whiteness. I couldn't move and my eyes seemed to be wandering around without being able to focus. Was I in some kind of coma? I could hear the voices of people approaching and tried to speak. Nothing. Was this real? Where was I? That terrifying question again - why couldn't I move or even speak? The figure of a man stood close by, dressed all in white. Then he spoke, I could hear him plainly; he spoke to me in Polish.

"Can you hear me?"

I desperately wanted to tell him, 'Yes, I can hear you!', but not only was I unable to make any sound, neither could I move my head or hand to signify that I could hear him. Fear washed over me and feelings of panic and with that the realisation that I must still be alive. The man, who I now presumed was some kind of doctor, lifted up my hand and tried to squeeze my fingers into a fist, but he could not move them. I wanted to help; perhaps if I could make a fist myself, he would realise that I am still here, still alive. There was another figure with him who leant forward and peered at me as if I was some alien specimen under a magnifying glass. I wanted to frown at him or somehow convey how I felt but nothing happened. The first man spoke again.

"I have never known anyone to recover from such serious injuries." He paused and then with a hint of optimism added, "But he is young, and we will keep on trying."

Then yes, I must be alive, but in what condition I could only guess. How long I might survive seemed to depend on how much I wanted to come back from wherever it was that I had gone. The next voices I heard were women. It sounded as if there might be a young nurse talking with an older woman.

"How long has he been unconscious?" the older one was asking.

'Ten days, Sister," whispered the younger voice. "He has brain damage; the Colonel thinks about a quarter of his brain has been damaged. He has quite a lot of scars from shrapnel wounds in his legs, shoulders, and neck as well."

"The poor boy," said the hushed older voice. "I will stay with him for a while and say some prayers." There was a momentary pause, during which I guessed that the older voice must be a nun, and then she prayed in a soft whisper, "O God, I commend this boy to your compassionate regard, knowing that no healing is too hard if it be your will. I therefore pray that you bless him with your loving care, and heal him, in your holy and precious name. Amen."

Amen! I wanted to shout.

There followed a period of time, I don't know if it was days or weeks, during which white-clothed figures came and went, speaking in hushed voices. In between, the enveloping blanket of darkness drew me down into oblivion, and I had no idea when I lost consciousness from my injuries or as part of my seemingly endless treatment. Later I learned that the Colonel, the surgeon who saved my life, had carried out twelve operations on me before he was satisfied with the treatment. I also learned that the first doses of penicillin were made available during the Monte Cassino campaign, and this had prevented infection after surgery. I wondered if it was the skill of the surgeon, the effectiveness of the antibiotics, or the prayers of the nuns that saved my life. Or was it that, from the outset, I would always tell myself 'Never say die'. I had many questions about where I was, where I had been, why I couldn't move and what the operations were for, but first I had to relearn how to speak. Eventually I was told that because of the damage to my head, the surgeon had to implant a platinum plate to protect my brain where the skull had been damaged. I did wonder what my head would look like with a great shiny metal patch on it.

"Don't worry," one of the nurses reassured me, and explained how the procedure would work. "The surgeon will put skin over the top, and your hair will be able to grow back."

My hospital stay lasted for nearly a year. Once all the operations had been completed, and my recovery began, I needed many months of rehabilitation and physiotherapy. It was not only my limbs that needed rehabilitation, but I also had to learn to speak, read, and write again. My memory also began gradually to return, often at unexpected moments when an event, or person, would suddenly come to mind in vivid pictures with all the associated sounds, smells, tastes, and emotions. It might be that a tune would suddenly come into my head and with it a memory of my mother playing the piano or father playing the violin. At another time, I would be given fruit to eat, and I would suddenly picture grandfather standing in his orchard with his honeybees. My childhood memories seemed to be strongest and returned first. I never did recover any memory of what happened just before I was wounded. It was only by talking events over, and other people reminding me of what had happened, that I was able to regain any memory of the battle.

Once I could read and write again, I was told that I should continue with my education. The greatest difficulty I had, after the initial recovery, was that I had lost my power of concentration.

"You must undertake intensive study," ordered the Colonel, the army surgeon in charge of my recovery. "My hope is that by doing so you will regain at least fifty percent of your previous intelligence level." Without knowing my educational background, I wasn't sure how he could realistically make this claim, but I gladly accepted his advice.

It wasn't long before I had read nearly all the library books provided by the nuns who nursed us. As I started to recover, and once I was mobile again, I looked around the hospital for something to occupy my mind. On the exercise ward, patients were attached to ropes and pulleys and there were some jolly chaps there. I made the acquaintance of these fellow patients, and we began to spend a lot of time playing cards and gambling away our army pay. Unfortunately for me, I had a run of bad luck and foolishly lost all my money. After that, I promised myself that I would never gamble again, however, I wasn't able to keep that promise to myself for long. As soon as I had saved up some more of my pay, I again joined the group who were gambling, committing the age-old folly of holding out the vain hope of recouping my earlier losses. Unsurprisingly, this did not work out, and it wasn't long before I had lost every lira in my pocket. Feeling foolish and angry with myself, I promised myself never again to play cards for money. This time I kept the promise to myself, and never did.

Instead, I decided to look out for some little job that I could do; some way to help out in the hospital, since the staff were always badly overworked, particularly after major battles, when the casualties would arrive at the hospital by the dozen. Our hospital was the biggest in the area, we even had anti-aircraft guns on the roof as it was such an important building. During hostilities, regular shifts were abandoned, and doctors and surgeons worked twenty-four hours at a stretch, while the sisters and nursing staff seemed to work non-stop.

Inevitably, our hospital had to deal with a lot of amputations, and I was allowed to watch several of these procedures. After I had watched a few of these operations, one of the nurses approached me with a weary smile.

"Would you like to help? We could use someone who isn't too squeamish to take away the parts of limbs that have been amputated, or other little jobs," she asked in a matter-of-fact way. I was surprised by the request but very glad to have some purpose; a way to help in this place that had already saved my life. By watching every day, I learned how to amputate part of a leg badly damaged by an anti-personnel landmine. One day the duty surgeon, who had been operating all day, called me over in the middle of an operation.

"I have no strength left," he said unashamedly, "I will not be able to saw through the bone of this patient. Would you be prepared to do this? Under supervision of course." Naturally I agreed and took up the required tool with some trepidation. It was hard work, but I followed the surgeon's careful instruction and completed the job successfully. After that, I was often allowed to help, and I think I became quite proficient with the saw. Thankfully, these procedures were all carried out under general anaesthetic.

The worst injuries, those ones that I found hardest to deal with, were patients with bullet wounds to their stomachs. I soon learned that these were very serious wounds from which few would recover. I hated the foul smell that would be released if the insides of their stomachs erupted. Apart from those, I found I could tolerate most of what I saw or was asked to do. But I must admit that I did not enjoy looking after patients who were coming round after anaesthetic, as, more often than not, they would be very sick, and also, tragically, many of them died because the operation had come too late, or their injuries were too serious.

The nuns, who were our nurses, were simply wonderful, and worked as hard as the doctors, doing a magnificent job. The wards were kept calm and peaceful. Somehow, they brought with them a sense of courage and peace, and they prayed with the men who were dying, regardless of whether the men had professed any faith or not. There was never any condemnation in their words or manner, only humility and deep compassion. For some reason the men liked being nursed by the nuns, perhaps because they felt that the prayers helped as much as the nursing care.

"Cakes!" announced Sister Maria, carrying a tray of delicious freshly baked cakes into the ward. "Just one each, mind, we don't want any gluttony here," she said with a gentle laugh. At the same time, one of the other sisters had arrived with a small, specially prepared meal for one of the patients who couldn't yet tolerate regulation hospital food. This kindness, though it might seem small, went above and beyond the call of duty, as we were treated more as if we were invited guests in a family home than patients in a hospital.

Sometimes, when the duty doctor was unsure how to record the cause of death of a soldier, there would have to be an autopsy. There was no red tape or strict control of personal data at the time, so we were allowed to watch these procedures from a distance. I admired the skill and precision with which the doctors carried out this work and began to wish that I could train as a doctor. However, although I was happy with the physical work, and the general idea, I knew that I would struggle to cope with seeing, or perhaps more truthfully, hearing them suffer, so I decided not to follow up the idea.

The medical and support staff in the hospital always seemed cheerful, and as I recovered my strength, I even began to enjoy my time in the hospital. We were able to listen to BBC radio broadcasts that were very informative, particularly if there was someone around who could translate. We even heard about fighting between the Germans and Poles in the forests of north-western Poland, which lifted our spirits thinking about home. There was great camaraderie and friendship amongst the patients on the wards, and with the staff. We were provided with many facilities and a surprising number of opportunities for entertainment. There were singers and dancers, and all types of entertainment, free of charge.

On one occasion, some of the other chaps were talking with great excitement about General Anders' military orchestra, the Polish Parade, that would be coming to the hospital to perform.

"I can't wait to set eyes on the beautiful Renata Bogdanska again," said one of the older men. "I saw her singing in a folk jazz band in Lwow before the war," he boasted.

"I saw her at Monte Cassino. It was just two days after we hoisted the flag over the monastery; she sang The Red Poppies on Monte Cassino. I was too far away to see if she truly is as beautiful as they say," chipped in another voice, "Anders' Polish Parade are not afraid to perform at the frontline," he added with evident Polish pride. Having left Poland whilst still too young to have much knowledge of such entertainers, I had no idea what to expect, and had hardly ever heard the kind of jazz or swing music that they were talking about. It was nothing like the music either of my parents had enjoyed playing, but I certainly thought they gave us wonderful performances and looked forward to the day I could learn to dance to a swing band with a sweetheart.

Eventually, in April of the following year, I left the hospital for three months convalescence in Noci, near the town of Bari, where the Allied forces had their headquarters. I really missed the smiling faces of the many friends that I had made amongst the hospital staff and other patients. Of course, the sisters and the ladies from the Polish Women's Auxiliary Service, known as the Pestki, who worked in the convalescent hospital, were also wonderful and I soon got to know them just as well. During my stay, we were taken on several outings, particularly to the town of Bari. There we visited the famous opera house, the Teatro Petruzelli, which had been requisitioned and occupied by the Allied forces to be a centre of entertainment for our troops. I was surprised to find that the entertainment was actually an opera called The Merry Widow. The theatre was packed. The Allied officers and local ladies, who dressed as if they were from the higher echelons of society, sat ensconced in the boxes all around. The lower ranks filled the stalls and lower tiers. The opera was a comedy, and the cigarette-smoke-filled auditorium felt a million miles away from the war-torn world outside its walls. There were also other theatres and many beautiful shops, and other sights to see such as the castle, cathedrals, basilicas, and the harbour. We were also taken to these other well-known places of interest and beauty in the locality. It was like a grand holiday although we were acutely aware that hostilities were still going on and our troops were still suffering and dying.

The climate was so warm in Noci that we would often sleep in the afternoon, like the locals, and then go to the beach in the early evening to swim. The sea was lovely and warm even until late at night. The warm water and swimming had a therapeutic effect on my wasted muscles and stiff joints. With all this good living, my hair grew back, and I put back on all the weight I had lost. I decided to pay a visit to the hospital that had saved my life. Hugely enjoying myself, I went shopping for small gifts for the doctors and other staff, and flowers for the nurses. I just wanted to be able to thank them for their many kindnesses whilst I had been in their care.

Loaded down with flowers and gifts, I hitched a lift in a military truck. I strode into the building with a beaming smile on my face and immediately spied Sister Maria walking purposefully towards me along the corridor. She smiled in response to the grin on my face but there seemed to be no recognition in her eyes.

"Can I help you?" she asked in her familiar kind voice. "Are you looking for staff or patients?"

"It's me!" I said, laughing at her evident confusion, "It's Viktor! I have come back to bring flowers and gifts to all my favourite doctors and nurses." Sister Maria took a step back and scrutinised my face as recognition began to dawn on her own.

"Viktor with the platinum plate!" she exclaimed. "So smart in your uniform, and with your hair all grown back; I didn't recognise you; you look so well." She then dragged me around the hospital helping me to find everyone for whom I had brought gifts and showing me off as if I were a trophy. It was wonderful, and I still treasure the memory of that visit that was so much like a home coming.

Whilst I was in Noci, I received an invitation to join a special unit, an Evidence Branch, that was being formed to assist with the repatriation of people who had been working as slave labour in German occupied territories, mainly people from eastern European countries, including Poland. There were hundreds of thousands of these workers from practically every country in Europe that had been occupied by Germany and including Germany itself. Since I could speak several European languages, besides Russian and Polish, I was given the opportunity to join this unit, and possibly also because they may have been unsure as to whether I would be fit to return to active service duties. So it was that I found myself working for the

United Nations Relief and Rehabilitation Administration, the UNRRA, as the war in Europe finally drew to an end.

CHAPTER 27

AUSTRIA AND GERMANY (1945)

By May, the exchange of Russian citizens and Allied prisoners of war had begun. Germany and Austria were each divided into zones of occupation, between the Soviets, the British, the Americans, and the French. I was sent to the border area between Austria and Germany to join a team to carry out Displaced Persons operations at the UNRRA assembly centre. These assembly centres were mostly former prisoner-of-war camps, army barracks, or former concentration camps. We were organised in small teams of four and tasked with locating people who had been forcibly taken from their home countries to work as slave labour and handing them to the UNRRA who would then organise their repatriation to their country of origin. It wasn't long before these Displaced Persons became known simply as DPs; from then it was a small step to them becoming mere numbers. Inevitably, each assembly centre's repatriation statistics came to be regarded as a sort of scoreboard to be compared with other repatriation camps. We were repeatedly asked,

"How many DPs have you repatriated this week?"

On arrival at the centre, we were given our simplistic instructions by the officer in charge of the centre.

"Your task is to find and collect DPs, arrange for them to come to the assembly centre, and we will organise their transport home," we were told by the organisers, who naively assumed that these people would want to go home. One man read out the wording from the UNRRA charter to remind us that we were not responsible for the actual repatriation, only for collecting evidence and locating people.

"It is not the function of the UNRRA to repatriate, or return to their former homes, persons, other than intruders, who do not desire such repatriation or return," he stated in a bored voice. I guess he had already become over familiar with the words.

At the time I didn't realise how important it would become to have the assurance of those words. In addition to locating DPs, we were also told to collect and record evidence of how these labourers had been treated. Looking back, I suppose this would have been evidence of possible war crimes.

My team started by visiting factory owners and then farmers, collecting details about the workers who had been brought in as forced labour, or had fled from war-torn areas or repressions of any sort. We made a record of their country of origin and their nationality. We then asked them if they wished to be repatriated to their homeland, and if so, we arranged for them to be sent to whichever assembly point would be best, depending on their nationality, from where they would be repatriated.

At the first interview, we gave these workers help with food and clothing. Unlike some of my team, I could readily empathise with these suffering people. Many of them were in a poor state of health and dressed in rags, but it was the hollow look of loss and hopelessness in their eyes that I understood most. I also understood the look of fear that transformed the features of some when repatriation was offered. I was thankful that I could remind the others in the team of the words of the UNRRA charter stating that it was not our function to repatriate persons who did not desire to return.

Some of the German farmers, perhaps because they were so short staffed, were very aggressive and refused to let us onto their property. There were also still some SS soldiers at large, who had not yet capitulated, who caused us trouble. As we approached a large farm, we suddenly heard gun shots close by.

"Down!" I yelled, dropping like a stone, and wriggling into the tall stalks of maize in the field alongside the dusty farm track that we had been following. The others quickly followed my lead. Someone was taking pot shots at us.

"What do we do now?" asked one of the men in a trembling voice; he had not yet seen active service and had evidently had a fright.

"We have no directives for this scenario," I said bluntly. "Our first priority is our own safety, and then we must report the incident and its location and leave it to the proper authorities."

"But how do we get away?" he wanted to know. I stood up and dusted myself down. By this time, I was confident that they had been just warning shots since there seemed to be no follow up; no one was making a search for us.

"That was just a warning," I said, reassuring the rest of the team. "If the authorities want to follow this up, they'll have to send in the military, after all it may be that there are a few SS holding up at the farm."

At times it was difficult work and sometimes dangerous, especially when the farm or factory owners tried to stop us carrying out our duties. We had to return regularly to our base in Italy to hand in our reports and collect fresh instructions. We had special authority to redirect or confiscate anything we needed for the care of the DPs.

There were, of course, many German and Austrian farmers who were quite friendly, and we were billeted with families with whom we got on with very well. Because we were staying on farms, there was usually a plentiful supply of home-cured ham, freshly laid eggs, and warm frothy milk from the cowshed. At that time there was a desperate shortage of labour. Many of their men had not yet returned from prisoner-of-war camps with the Western Allies, or the terrible Soviet camps, and of course many of them would never be going home. The men in our UNRRA team were all healthy young men that found themselves very attractive to the farmers' wives and daughters.

"You can marry my daughter and work on the farm," was the offer on so many of their lips, words that stirred some strange memories for me. We were happy to help with mending tools or with odd jobs, however, helping the local population was not part of our brief. Our concern was supposed to be the welfare of DPs and, perhaps more importantly to the authorities, their repatriation.

Whilst we were in the region near Lake Constance, we were making the usual enquiries, asking about people who may be eligible for repatriation. A young woman approached. Pointing to one particular house, and in a voice devoid of emotion, so that I couldn't decide if she meant to be helpful or spiteful, she spoke to me.

"The lady who lives in there speaks another language. She may know something; perhaps she can help you find what you are looking for."

I knocked on the heavy wooden door and waited. Eventually the door was opened by a diminutive late-middle-aged lady whose face broke into a beaming smile when she saw me. Addressing her in German, I introduced myself.

"Good day, excuse me for calling unannounced, but I was led to believe that you may be able to help. I am from Poland, but now I am working for the United Nations, helping with the search for displaced persons who may wish to be repatriated to their place of origin," I said in what I hoped was a pleasant and friendly manner. The lady peered up at me with an intense myopic gaze and then beckoned me into the house.

"Come in. Come in, young man," she said holding the door wide so that it would have been discourteous to have refused. "Now tell me, if you are Polish, how is it that you know German?" Having no reason to withhold this information, I replied with a touch of impatience.

"I learned German as a boy because my father wished me to have a good education, and also I think because my mother's mother, my grandmother, was from a German family; I have German ancestors," I told her honestly.

"You are still just a boy; a big boy," she said with a laugh. "Tell me, where in Poland are you from?"

"Rovno," I answered, "a small town in Volyn in Eastern Poland, close to the border with Soviet Ukraine," I added since it was highly unlikely that this lady would have much idea of the geography of Poland, and at the same time I wondered why she could possibly want to know. "My family were deported into Russia like so many others," I added by way of explanation. The lady grabbed hold of my arm and began asking me questions about all sorts of things. 'What is the matter with this woman?' I wondered to myself, 'Why does she want to know everything about me?'

"What about your grandfather?" she asked finally, "What was his name?" I had a momentary feeling of panic as if I had somehow fallen into a trap and was about to give myself away to some lurking NKVD agent. She could see my reluctance and realised she needed to ask a different kind of question. "Tell me." She said with barely concealed excitement in her voice, "What did he leave to you when he died?" I couldn't see how this question could be a trap; only my family would know the answer and it wasn't in any way something that could connect me to my father.

"His sword," I replied. All of a sudden, the little old lady was throwing her arms around me. She started kissing me and crying.

"What is it? What's the matter?" I asked, wondering what on earth was going on.

"We are related!" She said, still clasping me to her.

"What do you mean? How are we related?" I asked, utterly bewildered by the lady's strange behaviour.

"I am your grandmother," she stated, weeping with joy as she spoke. "Oh, my little Rudi! Never did I think I would ever see you again." I was completely shocked and asked myself if such a coincidence could truly happen. She tottered into an adjoining room and fetched out some old photographs. There was no doubt about it; this really was my grandmother.

Naturally, the first thing Grandma wanted to know was what had become of the rest of the family and how I came to be in Germany. I told her everything I knew as simply as I could without giving much detail and leaving her with the hope that her daughter and granddaughter had survived the deportation. But I was very curious as to her own story; how had she come from our home in Poland to be living here?

Like me, Grandma glossed over the details, explaining that when the German Army had occupied the region and were advancing further into Soviet territory, they had begun to move ethnic Germans out of the area, sending them to Germany, and this was where she had eventually settled. I was elated to have found a surviving member of my family, yet weirdly wary of what the implications might be; what risks this might bring to each of us.

After my first visit, I managed to arrange many more and often managed to spend the night with her at her house. There were many shortages after the war, so I made the most of my position and asked Grandma to let me know what she was short of. She asked for stockings, sugar, and all sorts of things.

"Leave it to me," I said, getting up to go, after that first and most memorable visit.

"Oh, my little boy," she said, clinging on to me and not wanting to let me go.

"Grandma, I am a sergeant. I have a job to do," I told her gently, promising to return as soon as possible with the things she had asked for. Each time I went to that area I went to visit Grandma and took her everything that I could get my hands on. She called me her little Rudi and asked me to stay. She wanted me to find a young lady locally to marry and settle down there to stay with them. But I was still in the Army, still on duty, and like so many other Poles still expecting something to happen to restore our homeland. In the meantime, my work continued with the UNRRA and the work of repatriation.

If we came across unaccompanied children, we were told that they would be considered as German unless we could prove otherwise. The difficulty for us was that children who had been kidnapped or orphaned early in the war had little or no memory of their country of origin and often had lost their mother tongue. It was heart-breaking if we could not find enough evidence to prove they were not German, because without it they were not eligible for UNRRA aid or repatriation. The whole subject of nationality for DPs caused great confusion. Some of the DPs used legal citizenship, others ethnicity, language, or even religion, as evidence of their nationality. To have Polish nationality, Polish ethnicity had to be proven and, in the confusion, the language spoken at home became an important marker for nationality. This made our work both difficult and frequently distressing for us as well as the DPs.

We had known for some time, since the Yalta Agreement was made public, that Moscow considered Poles from east of the Curzon Line to be Soviet citizens; that Soviet citizens were people who had been living in the regions that became Soviet-occupied territory as of September 1939, and that included me and my family. The Americans and the British did not recognise this territory as Soviet, but a cold chill went through me when I learned that the USSR had been permitted access to areas occupied by the Western Allies to repatriate Soviet citizens by force if necessary. It was as if a cold hand had reached inside and grasped hold of my heart. Was Grandma's family on their list I wondered. How far would they pursue us? Why couldn't we be left alone? I could answer all my own questions; I knew very well what it was that they wanted to keep secret and hidden from the eyes of the rest of the world.

When we were arranging for the repatriation of DPs originally from Russia, unsurprisingly, a great many of them did not want to return to the Soviet Union although the younger people, who had not been involved in politics, were usually anxious to return to their families. In southern Austria, there were anti-Soviet Russians who had fled the Soviet Union with the retreating German army. There were also many old émigrés who had left the former Russian Empire during the Bolshevik Revolution and subsequent civil war, as had my own father. There were also Ukrainians from what was Polish Galicia who had fought against the Red Army, and White Army veteran Cossacks. We heard that many thousands of these people were forcibly repatriated along with captured Soviet Soldiers by the Allied military. Rumours of their fate began to emerge and then eyewitness accounts of mass executions, deportations to Siberia, and imprisonment of those repatriated.

As these horror stories became widely known, the despair of those who were sentenced to repatriation led to suicides, others even begged the Allied soldiers to shoot them rather than be repatriated to the Soviet Union, and others seized weapons and tried to fight their way to freedom. Some of these suicides occurred at Kempten, a UNRRA assembly centre not far from where Grandma lived near Lake Constance. The Allied commanders began refusing to send Soviet prisoners of war and refugees back by force. Allied soldiers, including officers, helped with false papers, or by simply looking the other way.

Reporting back to base in Italy, I encountered a fellow who had been given the unenviable job of making decisions about who would be accepted as Polish citizens and who would be deemed Soviet citizens to be repatriated.

"Look, I have to make these decisions," he said with a hint of anger in his voice, betraying his sense of guilt. "We have to accept people who have all kinds of origins, German, Russian, Byelorussian, Ukrainian, we treat them as Polish citizens because they lived in our Republic. But some of these people, they are pretending to be Polish, but I can tell."

"What of these people, where do they go? Do you know what happens to them?" I asked tentatively.

"They will be shot," he said shrugging his shoulders. "It's not our responsibility. We have to do it, to make these difficult decisions," he added with a cold justification for himself.

We soon found out that the Soviets, not content with hunting down their own citizens, were determined to return all those considered by them to be Soviet citizens, including Poles. We heard reports of Soviet officers invading homes and entrapping people. At one of the DP assembly centres, armed non-uniformed Soviet officers forced their way in to kidnap three Polish women who they claimed were Soviet citizens, although the Red Cross had recognised them as Polish. One of the ladies managed to escape and go into hiding, but the other two were taken away and disappeared. These were not isolated incidents; there were many reports of people who had disappeared at their hands. We thought these Russians were NKVD, but later learned they were part of a new organisation known as SMERSH. This stood for Special Methods for Exposing Spies, otherwise known as 'Death to Spies'.

There were some Polish soldiers who had agreed to repatriation early on and had subsequently escaped from Soviet Poland and returned to Italy. They confirmed that the NKVD had stayed in Poland to combat our underground army, the AK, and guard the borders, and it was SMERSH that went to Germany and had a network of agents and groups that had been sent to hunt down the people that Stalin claimed as Soviet citizens. SMERSH operatives were seemingly allowed to roam freely, and there were reports that they resorted to kidnapping and even murder. It was believed that these SMERSH operatives had detailed lists of former White Russian officers. I wondered if there were lists with my family name on, a name that I had already kept secret for so long.

CHAPTER 28

ITALY AGAIN (1946)

When my special duties in Germany and Austria had come to an end, I returned to Italy to work as a Quartermaster Sergeant. I reported directly to my Commanding Officer with whom I shared an office. By this time, special camps had been organised by the UNRRA for the thousands of young Polish workers who had been used as forced labour in German-occupied territories, including Austria and Italy; there was an assembly centre at Bari. Those who were suitable for military service were drafted into branches of our Army and Airforce. At that time, we were still not sure what was going to happen in Poland after the war. We were still hoping, and even expecting, that the Allies would keep fighting on the eastern-European front and help us to drive the Soviets out of our homeland.

As Quartermaster Sergeant, I was responsible for the supply of food, clothing, and sleeping accommodation, receiving troops back from hospital, and despatching troops on educational courses at Matera where the cadet schools were. Worst of all, I was responsible for the pay roll every ten days. I had to work out how to change the money from British pounds, shillings, and pence into Italian lira. Every morning, we called our rollcall, said daily prayers, and issued orders for the day.

One of the biggest problems that now faced me, with my new responsibility, was the flourishing black market.

We were losing a great deal of military equipment and other supplies. Some of it was no doubt accidental loss, but much of it was being intentionally sold to the Italian civilians. Items such as socks, shirts, and blankets simply melted away. We knew that things were in short supply everywhere in Italy; food was scarce and for many the black market was seen as their only means of survival. Whilst trying to get an idea of how it was operating, I struck up a conversation with a local administrator.

"Only those who engage in the black market can live really well," he told me. "Many people travel from here to Naples in trucks and other vehicles in which they can transport goods. They take olive oil, macaroni, and flour with them. Then they exchange these and return with clothing and medicines which they can sell at exorbitant prices," he explained with a shrug of his shoulders. "The butchers are real crooks," he added with some asperity, "they keep back the best cuts of meat for illegal sale to make even more money." He seemed to feel personally aggrieved about this particular nefarious activity; I guess he was partial to those best cuts. Personally, I was more worried about medicines like the new penicillin going to civilians instead of troops at the front; there was only enough to treat our troops and I knew exactly how important it had been to my own recovery.

Many of the black marketeers were organised and professional, using the pilfering of our stores as an opportunity to make quick cash. What made it more difficult to deal with was that some of the Allied troops collaborated for the same reason. There were even reports of Allied deserters who stole food and clothing to hide from the Military Police and blend in with the locals. Although some of our soldiers got involved in the black market, mostly this was just selling items that actually belonged to them rather than misappropriation of military property. They exchanged their tinned or dried rations for fresh food, liquor, or laundry services. For these minor infringements there was nothing much to be done; the Commanding Officer and I had to be judge and jury. I supposed that given the dire economic circumstances, pilfering was inevitable. We had our own prison, and often it was necessary to lock men up with only bread and water, or for smaller offences they were confined to barracks. But we did have to instigate a special watch to guard the warehouses from armed gangs that began to target our supplies.

In addition to fostering the black market, the food shortages led to protests and riots. Some of the local people would attack lorries carrying food and break into bakeries to steal bread. As winter approached, the situation for many people worsened and a riot could start over a slice of bread. On one occasion, our troops had to be confined to barracks so that they wouldn't interfere or get caught up in the riots and make matters worse.

"There is a big crowd of men, women, and children rioting in the streets. They are looting the shops, wrecking businesses, and attacking police stations and government buildings. They have even threatened to lynch the city officials," we were told by an indignant and understandably shaken city official. "We have requested that the police use armoured cars and submachine guns; they have orders to fire into the crowd if necessary. It is most important that you confine your men to barracks," he demanded. In response, the Allied commanders decided to impose a curfew; although some of the local Italians saw non-compliance as an act of defiance against the occupying Allies which is what we had now become.

But far worse than dealing with the black market and food riots was having to tell our troops that the Second Corps would not be returning to Poland after the war. We had learned that the Yalta Agreement had led to the undeniable fact that Poland, our homeland, had been sacrificed to Russia on a plate through the complete ignorance of the Allied Commanders who believed that Stalin would allow free elections in Poland after the war. We had already heard rumours of this and of course we had heard what we assumed was German propaganda, and I for one had hoped that somehow it would not be true. After all, I asked myself, why would we have been recruiting new soldiers as we pushed forward through Italy, gathering up former prisoners of war, and Poles who had been forced to join the Wehrmacht, if not so that we could increase our forces in preparation for pushing the Russians back out of Poland? We were absolutely astonished that the politicians appeared to be completely hoodwinked by Stalin.

"How could the Allies not have known the situation in Soviet Ukraine when between the wars Stalin had systematically starved to death millions of people who didn't like his system of collective farming?" I ranted unnecessarily at my Commanding Officer who entirely shared my feelings.

"I can tell you," I added, fuelling my own sense of grievance as I raked up the past, "I visited some of my father's family in Ukraine shortly after the Soviets came and occupied our town. I saw what was happening on the farms, abandoned machinery, and abandoned fields. I was even told about the cannibalism which was happening amongst the starving population. It is too horrible to think about, but I believed the people who told me to have been speaking the truth." My C.O. silently nodded, sharing my bewilderment at the turn of events. After a moment of silent reflection, he shared his own thoughts and condemnation of the politicians.

"The Americans and British could easily claim ignorance, but our own politicians know how the Russians use falsified elections to give themselves legitimacy in occupation. But surely even Churchill must realise that Stalin plans to extend the Communist system all over Europe and maybe even over the whole world!"

When our unit heard that the decision had been made that we were to be sent to Britain, and that Poland would not be free of Russia after all their efforts, they simply went berserk. It was only by using strict military discipline that we were able to avert a riot. All soldiers had to be confined to barracks for several days. Many of the men, after suffering years of hardship and loss, and displaying such courage and bravery, wept tears of bitter disappointment on hearing that the military authorities could not guarantee their safety if they returned to their families in Poland.

In the optimistic belief that they might be able to form a nucleus in the Polish Army that would be ready to fight against the Russians, some of our troops decided they would return to their families regardless of the political situation. Others, especially in the higher ranks of the Polish Second Corps, continued to hope that Churchill would help us fight the Russians. There were rumours of such plans, of a secret operation, and our officers were desperate to keep us together, firmly believing that once Josef Stalin had subjugated the whole of central Europe, and thus become a clear and present enemy of the West, the Allies would again take up arms and re-establish a free Europe. The Polish Second Corps would then be willing and able to lead the attack.

Some of our lads nevertheless decided to return to their families in Poland. It was my job to equip the first batch to be repatriated.

"You will go as Polish soldiers," I told them, "Armed and in full military uniform." I equipped them with uniform and a rifle, and the necessary papers confirming their military history. They were then transported to the port to be shipped home. After the initial group had shipped out, others chose to go too. I was horrified to learn later that a great number of these soldiers never arrived. We heard that they had been classed as 'Enemies of the Soviet Union' because they had been serving with the Allies and had disappeared without trace. We were then instructed by the Provisional Government in Poland immediately to cease the repatriation, as they could not guarantee the safety of the troops involved. When I heard what had happened to the soldiers I had equipped to return home, picturing their weary home-sick faces, I became very depressed and could not sleep for weeks on end. My friend Captain Novak was one of those who, having gone back to Poland, simply disappeared.

"Poland has been sold down the drain to the Russians," a colleague told me with disgust. "I can accept almost anything that happens to me, but I don't want to be in the hands of those Communist liberators for a second time," he added, "Until Poland is vacated by the Russians and their Polish collaborators I can never go back."

I had my own struggles with this question. Of course, I wanted to go back, but the part of the country where I used to live had now been part of Soviet Ukraine for seven years. I had no family in the west of Poland to go home to. The Yalta Agreement had moved the borders of Poland from the east to the west of the country. My home, and my maternal grandparent's home, were now firmly within Russian territory. It would be impossible for me to visit them.

"I can't stand the Communists," I told him in reply, "I can't live anywhere that has Communists after all they have done to me, my family, and our people. I just can't stand them."

Whilst our own officers were bombarding us with political indoctrination, with Polish military and liaison officers spreading anti-repatriation feeling, warning us that neither Russians nor their Polish collaborators could be trusted to uphold even one of their pledges of our safety on return to Poland, we were also getting information directly from Poland. There were many soldiers who, having earlier decided to go back to Poland, had subsequently fled from Poland and found their way out through Czechoslovakia and Germany back to Italy where they gave eye-witness accounts of what was happening in Poland. There were also letters arriving from Poland telling the same stories.

To repatriate or not was a frequent discussion in our office; my Commanding Officer had family that he wanted to get back to.

"I can't stand living here away from my family," he said despondently, "but people who go just disappear, nobody seems to know what happened to them. One friend, with whom I had many conversations about this, decided to go. But I have since had a letter from a member of his family to say that he was accused of working against the state and has been executed," he added angrily. People said that they didn't know what happened to these people, but those of us who had experienced the methods of the NKVD could guess.

"I have thought about going, but my friends tell me 'For goodness' sake, don't go; you'll be arrested. If they know you escaped from the Russians, they will send you back to Siberia or worse'," I told him. "You know, as well as I do, that there is no freedom of the press, or freedom of speech. We both know that people disappear even for no reason. I for one will not be persuaded to go to that sort of Poland. No Sir!"

"We will have to wait for the right moment when we can return," said the C.O. with a flicker of optimism, "but we must wait until Poland is no longer a Soviet puppet. For now, we could have no say in political or economic life in Poland, just as it is in Russia; we can only return when the Russian Army leaves Poland."

To add insult to injury, the Russian authorities were broadcasting propaganda about the Poles who had escaped from Poland during the war and joined our First and Second Corps, calling them traitors who had sold themselves to the West for money. With all this going on and our continued inactivity, other than cadet training, our troops were getting despondent, despite the official line our Army Chiefs were still promoting, that we would soon be throwing the Red Army out of Poland. The non-commissioned officers were given the task of keeping the troops informed of the situation as a priority and had been instructed to inform them that the Allies now realised the grave mistake they had made at Yalta and would soon be doing something about it. Although we had to tell the men this, I could not find if in my heart to believe it.

The combination of inactivity and uncertainty as to the future led to further problems. Large numbers of our troops began to agitate against the information that was being passed down from the Polish Generals. The Polish High Command also needed assurances as to the future of the Polish Second Corps that seemed to me to have been left in limbo in Italy whilst the rest of Europe squabbled over Germany, Austria, and the Balkan States, and the Americans began to redeploy their troops to the Pacific war against Japan. Finally, we were told that the British Government had decided that the war was over, and we would no longer be required as a military force; we could do what we wished. We now realised that there was to be no liberation of Poland after all our efforts.

We were all given the opportunity to emigrate from Italy, including those who had already married Italian girls but chose not to stay. The countries offering relocation included Britain, the USA, Canada, Australia, New Zealand, South Africa, and France, or we could enlist with the British Army and go out to the Far East. I lay awake for hours on end, debating with myself which course of action I should take. Repatriation was out of the question for me. Finally, I decided that if Poland was to be free one day, then the closer I lived to it the better, so I decided to make England my future home. I realised it could be at least fifty years before I would be able to return and visit my old home, let alone lay claim to it, or my grandfather's home and lands to which I was heir.

When the time came to leave Italy, quite a few of the lads decided to stay there because they had enjoyed their life in that country so much. Although war torn, we had similar religious and cultural backgrounds to the Italians making us feel very much at home. Quite a few of our troops had already married into Italian families during the four years we were stationed there.

The country had also made me feel at home, with its culture and reminders of ancient civilisation. The only thing I really disliked was the rising power of the Communist Party. During hostilities, the Allies had secretly worked closely with the mainly Communist partisans, but now the threat of the spread of Communism led the Allied Commanders to seek closer relationships with those in Italian society who were more likely to be anti-communist. We had a great many clashes with the local Communist groups, and often destroyed their red flags and their hated pictures of Lenin and Stalin displayed in their shop windows.

After Mussolini had been removed from power, many of the communist prisoners of the former fascist state were released. They had returned to the Puglia and Basilicata regions and began to prepare for the reinstatement of the Communist Party. The Puglia region, especially around Bari, was known as the Zona Rossa, the red zone.

"These disturbances, that seem to be becoming more frequent, amongst the civilian population are surely instigated by communists," observed my C.O. "These vulgar troublemakers, agitating the rabble, are no doubt taking full advantage of the unstable political situation herc, using violence to try to gain power," he added. Although I had no personal experience of Italian communism, my own anti-communist feelings were barely repressed.

"When I see the people waving red flags in their street processions, I feel like a bull; you know as if it were a red rag to a bull as they say," I commented. But it was no joking matter, there had been violent clashes between communists and Italian soldiers. There had been groups of armed communists and violence in Matera, Bari and Foggia, and there had even been instances of Allied troops being shot at as they passed through towns under the control of communists.

Aside from the political and economic turmoil, Italy was a beautiful country. I was able to spend many hours visiting the art galleries and churches. I was able to visit Vatican City, Venice, and the ruins of Pompeii, and of course I had particularly enjoyed the months spent convalescing in Bari with its lovely opera house. Exploring in and around Matera, I was impressed to see how the farmers made use of discarded jeeps and military vehicles, Allied and German. They refurbished these abandoned vehicles, fitting the battered but intact shells with Italian-made engines to power them for ploughing and other farm work. The ancient part of Matera, known as the Sassi, was especially fascinating. Here there were ancient cave dwellings, where houses had long ago been built into the walls of a canyon so that only the front face of each house was visible, and these dwellings were still occupied. Barefoot children ran around the streets. Watching the local goat herder was one of the most memorable sights, a very different kind of milkman to the horse and cart I was used to. The goat herder would lead his nanny goat along the street and milk her directly into the pans and jugs held under her by the housewives. The vibrant images of the beauty of the landscape, with the small ancient towns nestling amongst the hills or at the foot of mountain ranges, has remained long in my memory.

A very different opportunity to get to know the Italian people arose when our Colonel-in-Chief invited me to act as his bodyguard when he visited the many aristocratic and wealthy families who befriended the Polish High Command. I spent many fascinating evenings attending dinner parties with him at wonderful villas and palaces, and medieval-looking castles. Of course, I was not allowed to drink any alcohol at these functions, as I had to keep an eye on the Colonel, but I was given a taste of the best of Italian cuisine. In fact, my time in Italy provided the social and cultural education that I had missed out on through leaving Poland at such an early age.

CHAPTER 29

ENGLAND (1947)

As we set sail from Italy, I was acutely aware that I was not going home as I had always expected, but I was going into exile. In 1947 I arrived on English soil. My first impression was of the grey bomb-damaged ports and towns of the southern coast. London had evidently taken the brunt of the war and the bombed-out landscape that had become familiar in the towns in Italy bore testimony to Britain's participation in the war. After the warm and sunny climate of southern Italy, the change in temperature was an initial shock and it seemed as if there was non-stop rain. But when, after having been moved around several times, I found myself in the camp just outside Kington in Herefordshire, the rain had ceased to bother me and I had acclimatised to the cooler temperature.

Although close to the border with Wales, the countryside was not of stunning mountain ranges, or of vast plains, neither were there ancient picturesque towns such as I had seen in the coastal regions of Italy. But to me it was simply beautiful. The war seemed hardly to have touched either the land or the people here. A peaceful calm shrouded the town and its surroundings from the turmoil in the rest of the world. The quiet only disturbed by the lowing of cows, bleating of sheep and an occasional vehicle slowly winding its way along the lanes. We were miles away from the next small town and even further from the one small city of Hereford. The camp on

Hergest Road had previously been used as a hospital by the American Army and had rows of concrete and brick huts for our accommodation. Not everyone at the camp was a Polish soldier, there were also Displaced Persons from Eastern Europe who were hoping to make a home in Britain. The local residents, especially the farmers, were very friendly and we had many invitations to visit homes and social events. In the summer, our boys even helped with bringing in the hay.

As the Polish Resettlement Corps, we were considered as enlisted in the British Army. We still wore uniform, but were unarmed, and our specific task was to prepare for civilian life in Britain. We were subject to British law and the King's regulations, but the military structure was still Polish, and we still had our Polish officers. The Ministry of Education was responsible for our education, and we were offered training in industries where there were shortages of labour such as mining, construction, heavy industry, and farming. There was every type of educational course available, from commercial to arts and crafts, all to get us ready for assimilation into civilian life. I decided against trying to get an office job, as I felt my lack of knowledge of the English language would be too much of a barrier. In the meantime, I was moved to York, then to Wales, and finally back to Herefordshire, this time to a camp on the Foxley Estate near Mansell Lacy village, just about seven miles from the city of Hereford.

Most of the Polish arrivals in Britain had no idea of the whereabouts of their loved ones, or knew even whether they were dead or alive, and that included me. Once we were settled in a camp somewhere we began the laborious process of trying to trace people. The newspaper that we had in Italy, the Polish Daily, came with us to Britain and they published appeals for information about lost relatives. I started searching for my mother and sister, hoping that they had survived the terrible conditions in Siberia. One of the ladies in the camp, waving her copy of the Polish Daily and reading aloud gave us some hope.

"It says here that the Provisional Government in Poland has been negotiating for the release and return of Polish civilians who were sent to Russia during the war; those who had been sent to Siberia and other parts of Russia."

"They are all communists," commented one of the chaps, "I don't trust anything that this Provisional Government says. They are all just Soviet puppets."

"There is probably a shortage of manual labour in Poland, where they need to rebuild, just as there is in the rest of Europe," I said. "It won't be out of consideration for the people that they are asking for this," I added.

"You are probably right," said the lady with the paper, "it says here that there are some areas like Kazakhstan where Polish prisoners have been forbidden to return home because they say they need them to rebuild that part of the country and work on the cooperative farms to replace the people they have lost." She paused as her own traumatic memories flitted across her face. "I had to leave some of my family behind in Kazakhstan. I will write letters, but what can you do?"

Holding on to the belief that my mother and sister were still alive somewhere, I continued my search for them through the Red Cross and various other channels, in the hope of gaining information on the repatriation of Polish people from the Russian camps. We heard that in parts of Siberia the Russian Army had recruited Poles to join their Army to fight the German invasion, and when the war ended the Russian authorities had given the families of these men permission to return home. It seemed that many others were freed from the camps but were left to find their own way back to Poland. As news drifted in about the thousands of Polish people who had perished in the Russian slave labour camps, we became increasingly despondent about the survival of our families. When the tragic and depressing news about the Katyn massacre broke I felt that I had even less hope of obtaining news of my mother, let alone of ever seeing her again.

Altogether, I had written about thirty letters to various organisations before I began to receive a few replies. I enjoyed the short stroll from the camp to the small village of Mansell Lacy where there was a post office. It was a strange old building that looked as if it was just somebody's house; somebody who kept pigeons. The whole of the front wall at one end of the building was full of pigeonholes. I wondered how long this had been a post office and if it dated back to a time when they used pigeon post. There was a straight road that ran right through the centre of the camp and directly into the village where it joined up with the main road to Hereford. It only took a few minutes to walk there, and I would deliberately walk slowly to get a good look at the black and white thatched cottages and square brick farmhouses and wonder what sort of house I might have one day and if it would ever be in Poland.

Eventually, the Polish Red Cross wrote to me to advise me that Polish former prisoners of the Soviet Union were making their way back into Poland and they would let me know if my mother's name was on the lists. I also received letters from the International Red Cross in Geneva that sent copies of lists of survivors, and they told me that they would continue to send fresh lists until I had been able to ascertain whether my mother was alive or dead. Another source I was able to tap into was the Polish underground, who by this time were known as the Home Army Resistance Movement in Krakow. They replied, letting me know that they would do everything possible to help me.

During my time at Foxley, a handful of us were secretly recruited for some kind of special operation, that we understood to have originally been at the request of Churchill himself, that required Russian-speaking Poles who had no known family ties and were known to have displayed courage; the type that was always first to volunteer. It was all very hush hush, and we were expecting to be sent into enemy territory at any moment. But in the end the operation was cancelled, and it came to nothing.

In the meantime, I received a letter from the Polish underground telling me that a lady with my mother's name had been interviewed by them in Krakow and that if I required further information about that person, I had to write to an address they gave me. I could barely write my next letter; my mind was in too much of a whirl and I tried unavailingly to remind myself that it might be a false alarm. I ran to the post office and felt as though I had been holding my breath the entire time when I received their next letter. I tore it open and read with utter delight and joy that this lady was in fact my mother. I could hardly believe my good fortune to have located her and that she had somehow survived and returned to Poland. My only sadness was that there was as yet no news of my sister.

It wasn't long before I received my first letter from my mother. I stared at the envelope for a long time before I opened it, trying to picture her face as I remembered it, imagining her sitting at her elegant writing desk and smiling at me. How foolish, I had no idea what her circumstances were now, what sort of place she was living in. The return address on the envelope was a place I had never heard of; a town called Olsztyn. I slowly opened the letter, wanting to make the moment last as long as possible. I drew out the single sheet of paper and looked at the spidery scrawl of the person who once had shown me such beautiful penmanship. The ink had run all over the page and I could only guess that it was from the tears that my mother must have shed whilst writing.

Not wanting any interruptions or inquisitive comments, I took the letter outside and walked into the densely wooded area that surrounded the camp on most sides. Leaning against a broad tree trunk I read that Mother had been unable to believe that I was still alive and found it even harder to understand how it was that I was in Britain in the West. I could tell from her letter that she was in difficulty; that she owned nothing and had no money. Carefully folding the letter, I put it back in the envelope and tucked it inside my uniform close to my heart and sauntered back to my hut. “I have a mother in Poland,” I told myself aloud.

As soon as I could organise it, I began to send parcels and money to my mother, but at the same time I began to plan to return to Poland now that I knew I had family there. Having packed up all of our belongings, several of us headed to the nearest port from where Poles could still be repatriated. I stowed all my luggage aboard and went back out on deck whilst the warning of some of my friends rang in my ears.

“Look, I understand that you think you should go to look after your poor old mother, but you can’t understand the danger you will face. It’s definitely not advisable for officers to go; you know that the Communist system will never trust people who are better educated; they won’t be able to convert you to their way of thinking,” said one of them, and I couldn’t argue with what he said. I stood looking down at the harbour, aware of the gentle swell under the boat. A feeling of claustrophobia began to steal over me. It started somewhere in the pit of my stomach, then my legs began to feel leaden, and a wave of adrenaline washed over me as real panic began to set in. At the very last moment I pushed my way down the gang plank and jumped for freedom. The boat sailed away with all my possessions on board, and I was forced to hitch hike my way back to the camp.

I had written to my mother telling her that I planned to return home to look after her. When I received her reply a short while later, I realised I had made the right decision on the boat; Mother had sent me an urgent reply telling me that I was never to go to Poland unless she herself told me it was completely safe.

"Stay where you are and fight for our country," she had written. "You have seen what the enemy can do to us and, therefore, you must never hope for salvation from Russia." From then on, I had to be content with sending her regular food parcels, clothing, and money, and I helped her in any way that I could.

The Foxley camp was well organised, with a cinema, scouts, a gym and the church. There was also a school for the children teaching Polish and English. We had our own Polish instructors here and could learn anything from woodwork, tailoring, blacksmithing, bakery, leatherwork, and anything we might need to equip us for civilian life. I found that I had a particular aptitude for tailoring and learned how to make trousers, shirts and jackets. An English Major Davenport owned the land, and we would often see his wife visiting some of the families. Our people often helped the local farmers which helped out with the food that was rationed.

My last base was in Wolverhampton, where I attended an Army School and took an open examination for entrance to a British University which I passed. There were some interesting moments while I was in Wolverhampton. The Polish secret services were operating in the area, contacting us exiles in an attempt to persuade us to return to Poland. They handed out pamphlets telling Poles of the good life to be had there. No one that I knew was tempted by this.

Before being used to house Poles and other DPs, the camp had been an airfield. An elite Dutch unit had also trained there. The locals would use the runways to learn to drive. On one occasion, some White Russians said that they had seen a Russian plane landing on the runway at night. Of course, no one believed their story, but there were rumours that a Russian civilian twin-engine plane had landed at least once to pick up a passenger with a suitcase, who must, it was generally believed, have been a Russian spy. The story went that a local bobby, wobbling along a lane on his police bicycle, happened to spot the plane and nearly fell off in his surprise. He made a note of the plane's registration in his notebook, and it turned out to be registered to a Russian civilian. Those of us with personal experience of the Russians were easily persuaded to believe the story was true; to us it was not so amusing. After this rumoured visit of what I took to be SMERSH operatives, I was looking forward to disappearing into British civilian society.

Having passed all my exams, I was sent to the north of England to be demobbed. I was given a suit and a hat for my entrance to civvie street. Fortunately, by this time I had already accumulated a few personal items in preparation for when I left the army. So, suddenly, after two years, it was no more army, now I must find a job and settle down. As an 'alien', I had to register my address and any change to it. I had to have an employment permit and carry a certificate of registration that had to be registered with the local police. My English was still poor, but I never had any problems; to me the English were always helpful and friendly. So, I found a job at an engineering firm in Birmingham.

At this time in England, everyone wanted to learn to dance, and Birmingham was full of dance schools. Everyone wanted to be able to do ballroom dancing and meet other people this way. I was persuaded to go for dance lessons at Hawley School of Dance. There were a lot of other beginners there every night of the week, so I didn't stand out, and quickly picked up the steps. This is where I met Mary, who happened to be a secretary at the engineering firm. Mary and I were married in January 1951, and we lived, as they say, happily ever after.

Viktor and Mary 1951

EPILOGUE

From my mother's letters, I gradually learned of her own journey from Siberia. When the 'amnesty' had been agreed, that allowed former Polish prisoners to be released, she was one of the many thousands who were simply freed from the camps but given no help with transport, food, or clothing, whilst finding their way back to Poland. When she set out from Siberia, the sum total of her belongings were tied up in a scarf. She had to beg for food on the journey. At times she was able to get lifts on transport lorries and at other times she was reduced to walking as she made her way back to our home in Rovno. Having made the long trek to Rovno, she sought out our home, only to find that it had been requisitioned by the Ukrainian Soviet government and was now being used for their offices. The authorities informed her that there would be no opportunity for her to remain in the town, and that she, along with other Poles, must leave immediately or risk being deported back to Siberia.

I could only imagine my mother's distress at having to leave her beautiful house in the hands of people that to us seemed mere criminals. Somehow, she managed to make her way to the western part of Poland, receiving help with sleeping accommodation and food on her journey from the churches she encountered en route.

Mother told me that as she travelled through the country that she could see the utter destruction that had taken place during the years of war and occupation. She made her way eventually to Krakow, in the south of Poland.

She arrived there dressed in rags, worn and fragile. She had made the journey alone and at this stage still had no idea if I had survived my journey from Siberia to Persia. She had never dared to let herself hope that she would ever see me again, because the journey I had planned to make during the early days of the war had been so dangerous; she had instead resigned herself to the idea of my death. My sister had long ago been taken away from the camp and sent to Moscow to be educated as a good Communist.

From Krakow, Mother was taken to be resettled in Olsztyn, a town in the north-east of Poland that had formerly been part of the old German area of Allenstein, and into which, during the war, the Germans had sent thousands of their own people. Now the German population was forcibly deported from this area to German territory. Those people like my mother who were expelled from the former Eastern Borderlands of Poland, the Kresy, were called Repatriates and sent to the area now referred to as the Recovered Territories. As elsewhere in Poland, the area had been devastated by the war, the infrastructure largely destroyed, there was rampant crime and gangs of looters roamed the streets at night.

After the evacuation of the Germans, Olsztyn became one of several large towns used to resettle civilians who had lost their homes in the eastern provinces to the new Russian settlers. Mother was given accommodation and promised a job as a teacher when the schools reopened.

My mother was desperate to find out if any members of our family had survived the years of war and deportation and went every day to the train station in Olsztyn. Every day trains arrived from the eastern provinces with families being resettled into the Recovered Territories that had been reallocated to them after losing their homes. One memorable day, to her great joy and surprise, my mother's only sister Hannah with her husband and children, arrived at the station. The family were, of course, overwhelmed with joy and relief to be reunited and they all decided to settle in Olsztyn and live together. When I received this news from my mother, I was also overjoyed and flooded with a sense of relief that now my mother was no longer on her own.

Several months later, I received more astounding news from my mother. It transpired that she had met up with my father's relations from Zaslaw in Russia, in Soviet Ukraine. This was the family that I had visited as a boy shortly after the war had started and after the Russians had invaded Poland, and with whom I had stayed for three weeks in their home.

Mother told me that father's cousin Joseph, who had been promoted to the rank of Colonel, had been made responsible for the supply of goods to the Red Army in Poland and East Germany, including Berlin. Huge convoys of lorries from Russia would travel to Germany via Olsztyn, and Joseph would accompany them as supervisor. The convoy usually stayed overnight at Olsztyn, where the men stayed in their vehicles, but the officers usually billeted themselves with families.

By a scarcely believable coincidence, Joseph had knocked on the door of my mother's family home, asking if he could stay overnight, and speaking in Polish. My mother and her sister's family were happy to let him in, offering him sleeping accommodation and a meal. As they sat talking together over supper, Joseph told them that he was from an old Polish family and that he lived in Zaslaw. My mother instantly thought of the family of my father's cousin, who were last known to be living in Zaslaw.

"We used to have relatives in Zaslaw," she told him, "But we don't know if they are still there."

"What is their family name?" Joseph had asked. When Mother told him, he was completely taken by surprise and couldn't believe what he had just been told. "You will not believe this," he said, evidently not sure if he could believe it himself, "I am the man; I am your husband's cousin Joseph!"

My Mother was understandably wary after all that she had been through and questioned him closely, asking him details that only someone in the family could possibly have known. Finally convinced of the truth of his story, my mother was then herself speechless with the shock of realisation.

"I have been searching in Rovno for any trace of the family with absolutely no success. No one knew anything about what had happened to you, and I had given up hope of ever hearing any news of you," Joseph told her, laughing at the surprising turn of events. Sadly, Joseph also had to tell Mother that after the war his wife Stella had been accused of being a collaborator and was murdered.

From then on, every time a transport convoy went through the town, which was, according to Mother, about once a week, she received all sorts of goods that were absolute lifesavers for the family. On one occasion, she received a hundred blankets, which at the time were worth their weight in gold. These were shared out between family and friends; they were dyed different colours and then cleverly made into thick warm coats. Another time, they received a truck full of fresh fish. It was far too much for one family and, being fresh, had to be eaten quickly. This also was shared amongst friends and neighbours. At other times they received items such as tinned food, and sugar, and various other commodities intended for the Red Army. My mother wrote that,

"My conscience is quite clear because we have suffered enough and they have taken away all our wealth, home and possessions, and this was just a very small compensation for our loss."

With all this news, I was both relieved and thrilled that my mother was now able to look after herself, and that she was being so resourceful that she was even able to help other people around her. The other good news was that Mother had at last received information about my sister. We learned that after she had been taken to Moscow for her education, that she had demonstrated her superior ability and was sent to train, and subsequently qualified, as a Doctor of Medicine. Later, she even became a heart surgeon. Because she was allowed to travel from Moscow to other Eastern European countries lecturing, she was able to visit Mother when she visited Poland.

My mother and sister had survived, and we knew where all the family were located and how they were. I sent Mother streptomycin with her food parcels because there were no antibiotics available in Poland at that time. In 1963, ten years after Joseph Stalin had died and many of the restrictions on travel were lifted, I decided to take the risk and finally visit my mother in Olsztyn. It is hard to describe our great joy in meeting after twenty-one long years; there was nothing but tears. The night that I arrived in Poland, none of us could sleep; we were so excited and talked and talked non-stop all night about our experiences and how we had survived.

I have to admit that we did not instantly recognise each other, after all, I had only been a boy when we were last together and by this time, I was well into my thirties and had been a battle-hardened soldier. Mother had also changed considerably; she had aged dramatically due to the hardship she had suffered during her life in Russia and the subsequent difficulties of life after the war. By the time I visited, she had lost much of the use of her arms and legs because of arthritis caused by all the years of heavy work in appalling conditions, with inadequate food, clothing, or medication. It seemed that it was only because of her strong constitution and will power that she had survived at all.

After my first visit, I proudly took my wife Mary to meet my family. We travelled there several times over the years by car, making the journey through Holland, West and East Germany, and into Poland. Olsztyn is in the lake district of the area and in time we were able to appreciate the beauty of the area where my family now called home. There was a time when I had hoped, eventually, when the political situation had improved, that we would have been able to visit my former home and the homes of my ancestors, but now as I approach my centenary, I know that story will never be, but I can still declare: 'Never say die!'

Viktor and Mary 2016

A copy of the next part of Mary's typed manuscript is given below:

<u>*Persia*</u>

There were several camps in Persia accumulating these groups of Polish Army prisoners of war as they were arriving, and I was sent to a camp in Paflewi [probably Pahlevi], *where I hoped to be accepted into the army. Officially I was too young to join the army, so as I had no papers, I gave my age as 17 instead of my real age of 15.* [I was originally told that Viktor was born in 1925 and then later they changed this to 1923]. *I was quite small and weak but despite these drawbacks I was accepted into a junior group, where we received general schooling.*

I was then drafted into a unit where I was given the job of camp barber. I had never cut anyone's hair before and certainly had to learn quickly. I was given a small tent, a pair of scissors and a chair for my clients and told to get on with it. I remembered from home how the barber had twiddled his scissors in his hands, and so, with trepidation, I twiddled my scissors reassuringly as I hoped, and attended to my first customer. My first client was concerned that I looked too young to be a barber and asked if I had received proper training. I replied, "You have to wait and see." The first results were terrible, and it took me so long to do that the chap nearly strangled me when he saw the results. He shouted that I was more suitable to be a butcher than a barber. He said he would have to wear his army cap for a month! The rumour went around to keep away from the barber, but when men were sent by the Sergeant for a haircut there was no alternative and I had to do it.

Later on, a very nice lady in our group who was a hairdresser before the war, showed me how to improve my handiwork. In fact, she could have been the camp barber, but she refused because the men coming into camp were suffering from severe skin problems and head lice, due to living in very poor conditions. I also learned to live with verbal abuse from my customers. I was really getting the hang of my job when we were all moved on to another camp.

On arriving at the next camp, I was given a job in the first aid room – my first aid box consisting only of aspirins and plasters. If anyone came along whom I thought was really ill, I had to book him in to see a doctor. I only had enough equipment to treat headaches and cuts and bruises. I was then getting fed up with being a camp nanny, and applied for transfer to military school, although I was still in the junior army unit. I was very anxious to make up for the education I had missed in Russia, and I finally passed all the examinations set at the army school. I then had the opportunity to be sent to college, as we had a lot of families with children who were far too young for military service, particularly mothers and children, and the army was educating them. Some of the families had even been sent as far as India to continue their educations. I refused this offer as I wished to join the full-time army as soon as possible.

In interview, Viktor told me:

"I was too young to join the regular army, so they made me a barber. Because everyone came with long hair – somebody had to cut the hair – they gave me the equipment – I was too weak to join the army. A chap came and cut someone's hair and said "see how I done it? That's how you have to do it with all the recruits." When the first chap came, I cut his hair and when he looked in the mirror, he nearly strangled me – and nobody would come to me – they said I was a butcher – I didn't mind. They all made such a fuss about their hair.

Luckily enough, people arrived who knew my father – many officers – they knew my father. So, they asked me what is your name? Where do you come from? What part? So that chap who knew my father went and told them who I am – you'll be surprised how it helps – it's not what you know but who you know.

So, they put me in an office. I had to register new recruits and issue their kit. That was alright – I was quite happy. But after a while of just sitting in the office I became jealous of the recruits who were marching and training – I wanted to fight. So, they put me in a unit to march, but that wasn't good enough – I wanted to be in a tank. So, I went to the chap who knew my father – he said, "Sit there; don't worry," and after about six months they had a place for me in a tank. I thought in a tank in a battle I'd survive. I decided I wanted to be in a tank because I thought I would survive better in a tank because it is protected. Little did I know how dangerous it was in a tank."

The Middle East

I continued my army training, going with our units to Iraq, where I was injured doing mountaineering training, and fell several dozens of feet with a full pack on my back. I had been lucky to catch on to a small bush which had broken my fall, but also at the same time broke my nose – my first military injury. On recovery I travelled with our units to Palestine, the Lebanon, Israel and our final training camp in Egypt. In Egypt I was most fortunate to be able to visit the most fascinating museums, see the sphinx and the pyramids, and become acquainted with the Arab people. The children were a constant nuisance begging for money. Egypt was then a very prosperous country, and the cities were a wonderful sight to my eyes starved for a long time of beautiful shops. The magnificent jewellery and the shop windows containing bars of gold for sale were a real shock to me. For the first time since leaving home I had money to spend and shops to spend it in. I bought myself a beautiful pair of leather shoes and also a few souvenirs. Many of the older men invested their army pay in gold coins, which they considered a good investment.

The training in the desert was very exhausting, as the daytime temperatures were over 100 degrees Fahrenheit, and during the night it was below freezing. We lived in tents, and the first thing we did on rising was to inspect our shoes, as they were a favourite hiding place for scorpions. I particularly hated the sand snakes, and the many other creepy crawlies, and the millions of flies which never left you in peace. At night we slept under mosquito nets, but I still had a minor bout of malaria. By now, I was training in a tank unit and the heat inside the tank was indescribable and almost unbearable, especially when we fired our weapons, when smoke was added to the heat inside the vehicle. The sand was hot enough to cook eggs on, and occasionally we had to endure sandstorms accompanied by electrical storms. From the distance you would see dark clouds of sand coming towards you, and when they arrived, quite large stones would be flung around with the clouds of sand. This would fill eyes, hair, teeth and even inside our clothing, which stuck to us with perspiration for most of the time. I often dreamed about our beautiful European climate and lush green trees and looking back I hated every minute I spent in Egypt.

Once we were trained, we had very little to do, and sometimes we were fortunate enough to be allowed to visit Alexandria, and although we were only allowed to stay in authorised lodgings, we were able to visit cinemas and clubs especially available to military personnel. Here we met army men from other countries, my first sight of British troops, the Australians, South Africans and Canadians, and, unfortunately, these groups of soldiers did on occasions aggravate each other and many fights broke out. Most of the fights were over petty things, such as some of the men putting their feet on the backs of the cinema seats; some of the fights in the clubs were quite serious, usually ending up with all the chairs and tables, glasses, etc. being broken and the army authorities having to pay for the damage. I believe this became quite a problem for the British authorities.

During this time, I was recruited into the military police and was sent for training in a Staff school, to acquaint myself with the paperwork and also to learn the legal requirements of the job. This was very time-consuming, the police records had to be precisely kept, as the records followed the troops around and had to be unbiased and strictly accurate. When the studies reached the stage that we covered the penalties to be paid by defaulting troops, including the death sentence by firing squad for desertion, I decided I could not possibly continue with this training, and I applied to go back into tanks.

Italy

In 1943 we embarked for the invasion of Italy. We were in the first prong which landed in Italy, where we were joined for the first time by American troops, whilst the second prong of our attack landed at Taranto. Whilst crossing the Mediterranean Sea our convoy was heavily attacked by the Luftwaffe, with bombs and machine gun fire. Several of our boats were sunk and we were unable to pick up many survivors. We were so crowded on these boats that it was standing room only, and we felt like sitting ducks awaiting our fate as the German planes circled around us. After landing at Taranto, I was transferred back to the special unit keeping personnel records in preparation for the heavy casualties we expected. Whenever we had a shortage of troops due to injury or deaths, I was transferred with other office and supporting staff into the fighting units again, and I received minor shrapnel injuries in tank skirmishes.

During our action in Italy life was very serious indeed and we were all under intense pressure, sometimes not sleeping properly for three nights. In the lulls between battles, we did try to enjoy ourselves. I remember once driving through a small town that had been heavily bombarded when we came across a wine store with the front window blown out and bottles of wine undamaged on the shelves of the shop. We stopped our tank, threw out half of our ammunition and replaced it with bottles of wine. We were lucky to get away with it, as this was a severe breach of discipline. We hoped that if we did have to fire our guns, the Tank Commander would not notice which tank was firing on full volume and which was not. We knew the American troops did this frequently, but we did it only once and considered ourselves very fortunate not to have been discovered.

One of the most nerve-wracking incidents for me in Italy was when a few tank crews were overrun by the Germans, and we were cut off behind enemy lines. We had no warning of their advance and we had to run off quickly without having time to prepare ourselves to fight – in any case there were not enough of us and we did not wish to be taken prisoners. Fourteen of us had to hide and had not been able to take much equipment with us, but we knew we were not far from our own troops and hoped they would soon retake the area without us being detected. We managed to evade capture for ten days, but our biggest problem was food.

The Germans had stripped most of the food in the area; in desperation we commandeered chickens and eggs from a local which he had been saving for his family. We left him a note to reclaim payment from the British Army when they arrived in the area. We divided ourselves into groups and hid in the cellars of the farm buildings. We made friends with one of the farmers and he decided one night to give us a glass of his best wine. He came into the cellar with a container and gave us a spoonful each of a jelly-like substance. We thought it looked very suspicious and he assured us that it was something only very special guests were given. We all ate a few spoonfuls and after ten minutes or so we began to feel rather queer, and then found to our horror that we could not stand up – our legs had turned to jelly. Then, we were absolutely sure that the farmer had found a way of disarming us in preparation to turn us over to the Germans – either that or he had poisoned us.

We called the farmer down to the cellar and when he arrived, we pointed our revolvers at him. He expressed surprise and asked what we were going to do with him. We said, "You have poisoned us, and we are going to kill you for this before we die." He burst into peals of laughter because he knew how the wine had affected us. He said it was very old wine – about 200 years – and from a special family recipe. As there was such a small quantity left, he only gave it to special visitors, and he assured us we would not die. We were still quite doubtful and kept him covered with our revolvers until we started to recover. We arranged between us that if we started to die, the last one alive would shoot the farmer!

After a couple of hours, we all recovered and regained the use of our legs. The poor farmer shook with fright for a few hours and told us he would never again give away his best wine, because he had sacrificed this, we had not appreciated it, and even threatened his life. He was most indignant.

We moved from his farmhouse in search of food and found an empty house. After investigating this and finding no Germans about, we located ourselves in the attic of the farmhouse. We made look-out holes and left traps downstairs to warn us if anyone came into the building. We stayed here for two days and ate all the food that had been left. During the second night we heard a noise downstairs and on investigation we found about six men had come into the building. They were searching around and as they could not find anyone, they made themselves comfortable in the kitchen and fell asleep.

We gave them a couple of hours to settle down and when all was quiet, we crept down from the attic to see who they were and how many. To our horror we found they were German soldiers. They must have been absolutely exhausted because they slept so heavily, they did not hear us and we stood looking down at them. One of them was a sergeant, another a member of the Medical Corps, and the rest privates. We checked to see if there were any more of them outside and, as the coast was clear, we woke them up and disarmed them. They could not believe that there was anyone else in the house. After we had disarmed them, they told us they thought some of their troops had played a joke on them, but we assured them we really were Polish troops. The Medical Corps man had come from the so-called Polish Corridor, near Gdansk and he spoke Kashubisz (the local dialect).

The Germans shared their rations with us, and this cheered us up no end. We had a further problem, however, to continue hiding ourselves and keeping the Germans prisoners. There was no point at all in killing them in cold blood. They were very nice chaps and caused us no trouble at all. They told us they would be glad when the war was over, and they could return to their families. One of them had been on the Eastern front and had been badly wounded before. He showed us photographs of his wife and children, and we all got very friendly with each other.

Later during that day, we heard the sound of gunfire getting closer and closer, and then shells started landing all around the farmhouse. Fortunately for us, it was the allied troops who were pushing the Germans back again. Our prisoners begged us to give them into the hands of the British Army because they had had quite enough fighting. When our troops reached our hiding place, we handed them over to the Military Police and they were taken to a place of safety. We then had to be returned to our unit, who had already posted us as 'missing behind enemy lines'.

During another confrontation with the Germans, we were heavily outnumbered and radioed for air support. This was to be provided by the American Air Force. To our great dismay the planes came over and, instead of bombing and strafing the German position, they bombed us instead and caused heavy casualties amongst our already weak position. After surviving that we were very dubious about calling for support, knowing that mistakes can be made, and the results can be absolutely devastating. As the front line changed so quickly it was difficult to pinpoint the area where help was needed.

Monte Cassino

Our Second Corps proceeded northwards through Italy until we arrived at the foothills of Mont Cassino, which was still under siege. This monastery had been bombed and shelled for many months, and several unsuccessful campaigns had been launches by the British, Canadian, and Indian armies against this stronghold of the German paratroopers, who had been given the task of halting the Allied invasion on the road to Rome. Many hundreds of dead bodies still lay scattered on the mountain sides below the Benedictine Monastery.

After many months of bloodshed and hardship it had been decided by the Army Chief of Staff that the Polish 2nd Corps, under the leadership of General Anders, would attempt yet another assault, and we made our preparations accordingly. Tanks had to be abandoned and all the troops had to ascend the mountains by foot. Somehow the Germans found out that the Polish army was taking over the attack, and we were assailed day and night by propaganda through loudspeakers and radio broadcasts by a female called 'Wanda' who spoke in Polish, desperately trying to demoralise us.

We were told we would be better off joining the German army as Britain would not help us in any case. We answered Wanda with bursts of machine gun fire. The Germans also dropped leaflets over our position printed in Polish, again telling us to 'give up, pick up a leaflet, join us and we promise we will repatriate you to Poland to join your family and you will be able to live in peace in your own country'. This propaganda enraged us all the more, and when we received our final briefing from General Anders on 5th May to commence the attack, we really were 'fighting mad'. The battle commenced with several hours of heavy artillery fire as we lay in waiting. It was absolutely deafening, and no one could hear any conversation or any other sounds. At zero hour, the very moment the guns ceased, we commenced our attack.

We had first to climb to the summit, carrying as many grenades as we could, together with machine guns and flame-throwing equipment. It was very difficult to flush out the Germans as they were in deep underground bunkers and had abandoned the Monastery buildings, or what was left of them. Our units attacked with great fury in revenge for the destruction of our homeland. After many hours struggling to the summit, our troops were able to destroy the Germans with grenades and flame-throwers and the Polish flag was hoisted on the ruins of the Monastery.

We lost hundreds of lives in this battle, but at last the Germans were dislodged and the road to Rome was open. A few German prisoners were taken and one of them later remarked that they were absolutely stunned by the ferocity and bravery of the units who took them. They thought we were invincible. From my unit of 120 men, only 17 survived. I was very lucky to survive the battle but had been seriously wounded in the head by a mortar shell and was transferred by plane to a Polish military hospital.

Hospital and convalescence

I was unconscious for ten days and my battle was certainly over. As I mentioned previously, I had received shrapnel wounds in my legs, shoulders and back during skirmishes, but these were superficial compared to the injury I received at Monte Cassino. I still have the scar on my forehead and top of the head to remind me of the action, and, whilst writing these notes, I am still having pieces of shrapnel removed from my legs some 50 years later.

My life was saved by a Polish Army surgeon, who carried out twelve operations before he was satisfied with his treatment. One quarter of my brain had been damaged, and he had to insert a platinum plate to protect my brain from the pressure of my damaged skull. I spent about one year in hospital; having such severe brain damage I had lost my memory and the use of my limbs. I could not speak or co-ordinate my eyes. I remember one awful occasion when the Colonel was examining me, he asked if I could hear him – strangely enough I could but could not move my head or hand to signify this. He lifted up my hand and tried to squeeze the fingers into a fist, but he could not move them. He turned to his assistant and said, "I have never known anyone recover from such serious injuries, but he is young, and we will keep on trying."

When I started to recover, I needed long periods of rehabilitation, learning to speak, read and write again, as well as physiotherapy with my limbs. When this had been achieved, I continued with my education. The Army surgeon had ordered that I must have intensive study, as by doing so he hoped I could return to at least 50% of my previous intelligence level. I had totally forgotten what had happened to me immediately prior to my injury, and only by talking events over, and people reminding me of what happened, was I able to regain my memory. The greatest difficulty I had following my recovery was that I had lost my power of concentration.

When I started to recover a little from my injury, I looked around the hospital for something to occupy my mind and some little jobs I could do. I had read nearly all the library books provided by the nuns who nursed us, and we spent a lot of time playing cards and gambling away our army pay. Unfortunately, I had a run of bad luck and lost all my money and promised myself that I would never gamble again. However, as soon as I had saved up a little more of my pay, I again joined the gambling group, hoping this time to recoup my earlier losses. This did not work out and very soon I had lost every lira in my pocket. This time I got very angry with myself and promised, once again, never to play cards for money. This time I kept my promise, and to this day, fifty years later, I have not played a single card game for cash.

I decided then that I would help out in the hospital, as the staff were always badly overworked, particularly after large battles, when the casualties came into the hospital in dozens at a time. Our particular hospital dealt with a lot of amputations, and I watched several of these operations. To my surprise, after a time I was allowed to help with little odd jobs, such as taking away the parts of the body that had been amputated, i.e., legs or arms. By watching every day, I knew how to amputate part of a leg badly damaged by landmines, and one day the surgeon allowed me to cut off part of a patient's leg, under supervision of course. The surgeon had been operating all day and was physically too tired to saw through the bone of the last patient. After completing this successfully, I was often allowed to help out, and became quite proficient with my saw. The only injuries I really hated were patients with bullet wounds in their stomachs. These were very serious wounds from which very few recovered. I hated the smell when the insides of their stomachs erupted. I got to be able to tolerate many things, but I did not enjoy looking after patients who were coming round from anaesthetic and became very sick, and many of them died because the operation came too late, or the injuries were too serious.

The nuns who acted as nurses were simply wonderful and worked as hard as the doctors. They brought courage and peace and prayed with the dying men. For some reason the men liked being nursed by the nuns because they felt that their prayers helped as much as the actual nursing. In other ways the nuns were very kind to us. They baked special cakes for us, and cooked other small meals for the invalids. We only had to pay for the ingredients as this was not regulation hospital food.

On a few occasions the doctors had to perform an autopsy, for example, if they were not sure how the soldier had died. We were allowed to watch this from a distance – as nothing in the army was secret. We admired the skill and precision with which the doctors carried out their work and I began to wish that I was a doctor. I liked the physical work but did not like to see patients suffer, so I decided against following this idea.

The medical staff were always very cheerful and after recovering to a certain extent I even enjoyed my time in hospital because of the comradeship and friendship the military hospital provided. There were many amenities and entertainments provided. We had concerts, and on occasions, General Anders' personal military orchestra came along and gave us wonderful musical performances. We had singers and dancers, and all types of entertainment provided free of charge.

When I left the hospital for three months' convalescence in Noci, I really missed the smiling faces of the many friends I had made amongst the hospital staff. At the end of my convalescence period, I paid them a visit taking along flowers for the nurses and small gifts I had been able to buy for the doctors and other staff – just to thank them for their many kindnesses whilst I had been in hospital. When I arrived, they could not recognise me, as I was dressed in uniform, my hair had regrown, and I had put on all the weight I had lost whilst ill. They were absolutely delighted with the improvement in my health and very pleased I had called back to see them all.

During my convalescence we were taken on several outings, particularly to the town of Bari, where we visited the famous Opera House, the many theatres and beautiful shops. As well as Bari, we were taken to other well-known places of interest and beauty in the locality. It was so warm in Noci that we often used to sleep during the daytime and go to the beach in the early evening to swim, as the sea was very warm until quite late in the night.

Whilst in Noci I received an invitation to join a special unit which was being formed to prepare for the repatriation of slave labour after the war. There were thousands of these workers from practically every country in Europe occupied by Germany.

As I could speak one or more central European languages, besides Russian and Polish, I was given the opportunity to join the Evidence Branch, particularly as it was thought I may not be fit to return to active service duties.

Austria and Germany

Shortly after I joined this unit, the war finished and we started visiting farmers and factory owners in Germany and Austria, recording evidence from the workers as to how they had been treated. We took details of their country of origin, asked if they wished to be repatriated to their homeland, and then arranged for them to be sent to central points, depending on their nationality, from where they would be repatriated.

At the initial interview, these workers had to be given help with food and clothing, as many of them were in a poor state of health and dressed in rags. Some of the German farmers were very aggressive and refused to let us on to their property, and we even had guns fired at us. It was difficult work and sometimes dangerous, as at this time the German SS had still not capitulated and were even trying to prevent us going about our work. We worked in groups of four for safety and had to return to Italy regularly in order to hand in our reports and collect fresh instructions. We had special authority to redirect or confiscate anything we needed for the care of the slave labourers, who were later designated as Displaced Persons (DPs).

Many of the German and Austrian farmers were quite friendly, and we were billeted with families with whom we got on very well indeed. They were desperately short of labour, as their menfolk had not yet returned either from prisoner-of-war camps with the western allies, or the terrible camps in Russia. One or two of the farmers' wives wanted some of our boys to stay and marry their daughters and work on the farm with them.

When we were arranging for the repatriation of the workers from Russia, a great many of them did not want to return and we even had some who committed suicide rather than return to the Soviet Union, where they had suffered such hardships before the war began. It was mostly the younger people who had not been involved in politics who were anxious to return to their families.

In interview, Viktor told me:

"Because I knew languages, they sent me to Germany to help organise the repatriation of forced labour of eastern Europeans including Russians. There were about two million Russians in Germany. The United Nations organised sending the people home. They sent me to Germany, and we had to organise transport back to Russia. I had to organise papers for many people. The KGB threatened us to try to get all the people repatriated – not everyone wanted to go back. But the UN were organising transport back, not the army. But we had to collect them and send them home. It wasn't our job to make them go.

While I was looking and asking where people were, I was directed to one particular house where a lady lived who spoke another language. So, I went to that house and introduced myself and she was asking me how I knew German. I said I had ancestors from Germany. She kept asking me questions, all sorts of things – I thought, 'what is the matter with you? You want to know everything about me.' All of a sudden, she put her arms around me and started kissing me and crying – this old lady – I said, "what's the matter?" She said, "we're related," I asked "How?" and she started to tell me all about it – I was so shocked, she was my grandmother! She started fetching old photographs and then I accepted that she was my grandmother.

Of course, there were shortages after the war, but I could supply anything – I was a real power over there – I was in the army and could get anything, so I asked her what she was short of. She wanted stockings, sugar, and all sorts of things. I said leave it to me. She didn't want to release me when it was time to go – she called me her little boy – I was a sergeant. I said, "Grandma I have a job to do." Each time I went to the area I went to see grandma. I got her everything I could get. She wanted me to find a young lady locally so that I would stay with them. I said, "Grandma I am still on duty." She called me Rudi, "Oh my little Rudi". I spent many nights staying with her."

Italy again

Special camps were organised for the thousands of young Polish workers and those suitable for military service were drafted into branches of our Army and Airforce, as we were not sure what was going to happen in Poland after the war.

Following the termination of these special duties in Germany and Austria I returned to Italy to work as a Quarter Master Sergeant, reporting directly to a Commanding Officer, with whom I shared an office. I was responsible for the supply of food, clothing and sleeping accommodation, receiving troops back from hospital, despatching troops on educational courses, etc, and worst of all, the pay roll every ten days.

Our greatest problem was the loss of so much military equipment, either accidentally, or intentionally being sold to the Italian civilians for their flourishing black market. Such things as socks, shirts and blankets simply melted away. For minor offences, the C.O. and I had to be judge and jury; we had our own prison, and often it was necessary to lock men up with only bread and water, or for smaller offences they were confined to barracks. Every morning we called our rollcall, said daily prayers, and issued orders for the day.

Our worst experience was when we had to tell the troops that the Second Corps would not be returning to Poland after the war. Following the Yalta agreement, and the undeniable fact that Poland had been sacrificed to Russia on a plate, through the complete ignorance of the Allied Commanders in believing that Stalin would allow free elections in Poland after the war. We were absolutely astonished that the politicians appeared to be completely hoodwinked by Stalin. How could the Allies not have known the situation in the Ukraine when, during the years 1933 to 1938, Stalin systematically starved to death eight million people, who he thought would not cooperate with his system of collective farms, just as one example? When I visited our family in the Ukraine in 1940, I had been told of the cannibalism which occurred amongst the starving population, the details too horrible to write about. Surely our politicians must have realised that Lenin's plan was to extend the Communist system all over Europe, and hopefully, the world!

Our unit, on hearing the decision that we were to return to Britain, and that Poland would not be free of Russia after all their efforts, simply went berserk. It was only strict military discipline which prevented a riot. All soldiers had to be confined to barracks for several days. Many of the men, after many years of hardship and great bravery, wept tears of bitter disappointment on hearing that the Military Authorities could not guarantee their safety if they returned to their families in Poland.

A few months after the end of the war many of our colleagues decided they would return to their families, regardless of the political situation. The military establishment of the Polish 2nd Corps was almost desperate to keep us all together, as they firmly believed that once Joseph Stalin had subjected the whole of central Europe, and thus become an enemy of the West, the Allies would again take up arms and re-establish a free Europe – and the 2nd Corps would then be able and very willing to lead the attack. However, as things turned out, Messrs Churchill and Truman decided that they could do nothing, and the famous term 'Cold War' was coined by Churchill on one of his visits to the USA.

Whilst we were being bombarded with political indoctrination from our own officers, we were getting information from Poland that the Russian authorities were broadcasting propaganda about the Poles who had escaped from Poland during the war and joined the Polish 1st and 2nd Corps – calling them traitors who had sold themselves to the West for money.

All in all, very many of our troops were getting despondent, despite the official line our Army Chiefs were promoting, that we would soon be throwing the Red Army out of Poland. The NCOs were given a priority task of keeping the troops informed of the situation and had been instructed to inform them that the Allies now realised the grave mistake they had made at Yalta and would soon be doing something about it. Although we had to tell the men this, I could not find it in my heart to believe it.

As time went by another problem arose with a large number of troops who started to agitate against the information passed down from the Polish generals, and so the matter was taken up officially with the British High Command. After a short while we were told that the British government had stated that, "The war was over, and we were not required any further, and we could do what we wished." We were all then given the opportunity to emigrate from Italy to many countries, amongst them Britain, USA, Canada, Australia, New Zealand, South Africa and France – or join the British Army and go out to the Far East.

After this ultimatum, our lads began to disperse. Quite a few had decided to return to their families, and I had to equip the first batch of 17 to be repatriated to Poland. I equipped them with full military uniform and a rifle, the necessary papers confirming their military history, etc., and we despatched them to the port to go home. After this initial group returned, very many others did too, but we later heard that a great number of them never arrived. They were classed as 'Enemies of the Soviet Union' for serving with the Allies. Soon after, we were instructed by the Polish Government to immediately cease this repatriation, as they could not guarantee the safety of the troops involved.

When I heard what had happened to the colleagues, I had equipped to return home, I became very depressed and could not sleep for weeks on end. I realised that we were going to be exiles for many years, if not permanently. Whilst lying awake for hours on end, I decided that, if Poland was to be free one day, then the closer I lived to it the better, so I decided to make England my future home.

Unfortunately for me personally, the Yalta Agreement had moved the borders of Poland from the East to the West of the country. My home and my maternal grandparent's home were now firmly within Russian territories, and it would be impossible for me to visit them, as they were in a part of Russia unavailable to tourist or any visitors from abroad. I realised that it could be 50 years before I would be able to even visit my old home, let alone lay claim to it, and my grandfather's home and lands, to which I was heir.

When the time came to leave Italy, quite a few of the lads decided to stay there, because we had enjoyed our life in that (though war-torn) country. We had similar religious and cultural backgrounds as the Italians and quite a few of the troops had married into Italian families during the four years we were stationed there.

From my point of view, the only thing I disliked in Italy was the rising power of the Communist Party. We had a great many clashes with the local Communist groups, and often destroyed their red flags and pictures of Lenin and Stalin displayed in their shop windows.

I had loved the countryside of Northern Italy, and spent many hours visiting art galleries, churches, Vatican City, Venice, and the ruins of Pompeii etc., and had particularly enjoyed the three months' convalescence I spent near Bari, with its lovely opera house. Another opportunity to get to know the Italians arose when our Colonel-in-Chief had invited me to act as his bodyguard when he visited the many aristocratic and wealthy families who had befriended the Polish High Command. I spent many fascinating evenings attending dinner parties with him at wonderful villas and palaces. I was not allowed to drink at these functions, as I had to keep an eye on the Colonel. In fact, Italy provided the social and cultural education I had missed through leaving Poland at such an early age.

England

In 1947 I arrived in London, and from there we were moved around the countryside to several army camps in different parts of Britain. My favourite was Kington in Herefordshire. The countryside was simply beautiful and the residents, especially the farmers, were very friendly and we had many invitations to visit homes and social events. In the summer, our boys helped with haymaking, anything to fill in the days whilst we were waiting to be demobbed. Every type of educational course was held in Kington barracks, anything from commercial activities to craft training – to fit us for civilian life. I decided against an office job, as I felt my lack of knowledge of the English language would be a great barrier. I was moved to York, and then to Wales, and finally ended up at a camp on the Foxley Estate in Herefordshire. We had our own Polish instructors here and could learn anything from woodwork, tailoring, blacksmithing, bakery, leatherwork, in fact, anything to equip us for civilian life.

My last base was in Wolverhampton, where I attended and Army School and took an open examination for entrance to a British university, which I passed – and was then sent to the north of England to be demobbed. I was given a suit and a hat for my entrance to civvie street – fortunately I had already accumulated a few personal items in preparation for when I left the army.

In interview Viktor told me:

"I went on a boat to go back to Poland. But at the last minute I changed my mind. I jumped of the boat but had left all my possessions on board because there wasn't time to get them. Other people on that boat disappeared when they got to Poland. My friend Captain Nowak went back to Poland and disappeared.

I met Mary at Hawley's Dance Class in Birmingham. We were married in 1951."

Immediately after the war ended, I started searching for my mother and sister, hoping that they had survived their harsh treatment in Siberia. We had heard that the recently formed Communist Government in Poland had been negotiating for the release and return of the thousands and thousands of civilians sent to Russia during the war, who had been sent to many parts of Russia as well as Siberia. Some areas, like Kazakhstan, for example, had forbidden prisoners to return home, as they needed them to rebuild the country and work on co-operative farms, to replace their won people who had been scattered all over Europe. In many parts of Siberia, the Russian Army had recruited young Poles to join their army to fight the German invasion, and when the war ended the Russian authorities had given the families of these men permission to return home. Many others were freed from the camps, but were given no help with transport, food or clothing to find their way back to Poland. My mother came into this category, and she left Siberia with her total belongings tied up in a scarf; she had to beg for food on the journey. She made her way back to our house in Rovno by walking and lifts on transport lorries. When she arrived, she went to our home, only to find it had been designated a government building and was being used as an office. She was told by the authorities that there would be no opportunity for her to remain in the town and she must leave immediately, or she would be returned to Siberia. She then made her way to the western part of Poland, and on her journey she received help from the churches en route with sleeping accommodation and food.

The situation in Poland after the war was a thousand times worse than the position Germany found herself in. The country had been almost totally destroyed. My mother finally made her way to Krakow, in the south of Poland. She was completely dressed in rags and looked very worn and fragile. She had made the journey alone, as my sister had been taken away from the camp and sent to Moscow to be educated as a good Communist. My mother did not know at this stage that I had survived my journey from Siberia to Persia and she told me later that she had never dared to hope to ever see me again, because the journey I had made during the early days of the war was very dangerous, and because of this she had resigned herself to my death.

In the meantime, I continued searching for her through the Red Cross and various other channels in the hope of gaining information on the repatriation of Polish people from the Russian camps. I also assumed that my mother had lost her life, especially on hearing of the thousands and thousands of Polish civilians who had perished in Russian labour and extermination camps – we were all very depressed on hearing of the Katyn massacre of Polish officers and all in all I had not got very high hopes of obtaining news of her, let alone ever seeing her again. Our people were regarded by the Russian authorities as the 'Capitalist enemies of the Soviet State' and had to be destroyed in order to continue the existence of Communist Russia.

Altogether I had written about thirty letters to various organisations and started to receive a few replies. Eventually, the Polish Red Cross wrote to advise me that prisoners were making their way back into Poland and they would let me know if my mother's name was on the lists. In addition, I received information from the International Red Cross, Geneva, with lists of names of survivors and they advised me they would continue to send fresh lists until I had ascertained whether my mother was alive or dead. Another source I had contacted was the Polish Underground Army (called AK) in Krakow, [By 1945 it was called the Home Army Resistance Movement ROAK] and they had replied to the effect that they would do everything possible to help me. Finally, I received a letter from AK telling me that a lady with my mother's name had been interviewed by them in Krakow. If I required further information about that person, then I had to write to an address they gave me.

Imagine my great delight and joy when I found this was my mother. I could not believe my great good fortune that she had survived and returned to Poland. I received a letter from her, and that letter had evidently been wet with her tears, as the ink had run all over it. She told me that she could not believe that I was still alive and in the West. I knew that she was in terrible trouble having absolutely nothing and I immediately sent her parcels and money to help her. I wrote to ask if I could return home to look after her and she sent an urgent reply that I was never to do that until she herself told me it was completely safe. "Stay where you are and fight for our country," she wrote, "you have seen what the enemy can do to us, and, therefore, you must never hope for salvation from Russia." From then on I was able to send her regular food parcels, clothing and money, and helped in every way that I could.

Epilogue

My mother was finally resettled in Olsztyn, a town in the northeast that had been part of the old German area of Allenstein and into which, during the war, the Germans had sent thousands of their own people. When the Germans evacuated Poland at the end of the war, this town was one of several large towns to resettle civilians who had lost their homes in the eastern provinces to the new Russian settlers. She was given accommodation and promised a job as a teacher when the schools reopened.

Every day in Olsztyn trains arrived from the eastern provinces with families being resettled into the area reallocated to them after losing their homes. My mother went to the station every day to see if other members of her family had managed to survive and were also being allocated to this area. To her great joy, her only sister Hannah and her husband and children, were on one of the arrivals. The family were overjoyed to be reunited and they all decided to settle in Olsztyn and live together. I was overjoyed to hear this news, as I then knew my mother was not on her own anymore.

Several months later, I was absolutely astounded to hear from my mother that she had met up with our relatives from Zaslaw, Russia. This was the family I had visited immediately after the war had started and with whom I had stayed for three weeks in their home. It happened like this – Joseph, who had been promoted to the rank of Colonel, had been made responsible for the supply of goods to the Red Army in Poland and Germany – up to and including Berlin. He used to accompany huge convoys of lorries from Russia to Germany, via Olsztyn, where they usually stayed overnight – the men in their vehicles and the officers usually billeted themselves with families. By the greatest coincidence, Joseph had knocked on the door of the family home, asking if he could stay overnight, and speaking in Polish. They, of course, let him in, and when talking, he told them he was from Polish stock and lived in Zaslaw. My mother told him that we used to have relatives in Zaslaw. He asked for their name and when mother told him he nearly fainted with shock and answered, "I am the man who is your relative". My mother questioned him closely and after being convinced that this really was a relation, she herself became speechless with shock. He told her he had been searching in Rovno for any trace of us but without success. No one knew what had happened to us.

From then on, every time a transport went through Olsztyn, which was about once a week, she received all sorts of goods which were absolute lifesavers for the family. Once, she received 100 blankets, which then were worth their weight in gold. People dyed them and made them into coats. Another time she received half-a-lorry full of fresh fish, which was far too much for the family as it had to be eaten quickly, so this was divided between friends and neighbours. At other times she received tinned food, sugar, and various commodities needed for the Red Army. My mother told me, "My conscience is quite clear because we have suffered enough and they have taken away all our wealth, home and possessions, and this was just a very small compensation for our loss."

I was really thrilled that at last she could look after herself, and being so resourceful, she was even helping other people around her. In the meantime, my mother had received news of my sister. She had been taken to Moscow for her education and being absolutely brilliant she had qualified as a Doctor of Medicine, and later as a surgeon. She then travelled from Moscow to other Eastern European countries lecturing and was able to visit our mother when she visited Poland. So, we knew where all the family was located and how they were.

When, in 1963, Joseph Stalin died and restrictions on travel were raised, I took the plunge and visited my mother in Olsztyn. Imagine our great joy in meeting after 21 years – we did not instantly recognise each other, because I was a mere boy when I last saw her, and I was now well into my thirties. My mother had aged dramatically due to the hardship of her life in Russia and subsequently the difficulties of life after the war. When I saw her, she had almost lost the use of her arms and legs – due to arthritis caused by heavy work for years, without adequate food, clothing, or medication. It was only because of her strong constitution and will power that she had survived at all. The night I arrived in Poland, none of us could sleep – we were so excited and talked and talked non-stop about our experiences and how we survived.

In Interview Viktor told me:

"Mother survived. I saw her after the war; there was nothing but tears. I sent her streptomycin as there were no antibiotics available in Poland, and food parcels. The family home was in Russia after the war, and everything was lost. Mother went to live in Olsztyn by the lakes; the lake district, where a lot of Germans lived before the war who were sent back afterwards. I traced her through the Red Cross. She had tuberculosis; we sent her antibiotics through a firm in London. Aunt Stella was murdered because they thought she was my father's sister. My sister became a heart specialist. She died of TB in her forties; she never married."

After my first visit, I took my wife to meet my family, and we travelled there for many years by car, making the journey through Holland, West and East Germany, into Poland. I hope eventually, when the political situation improves that we will be able to visit my former home and the home of my grandfather, but that will be another story...

POSTSCRIPT

MY OWN JOURNEY AS AUTHOR

In 1997, my parents moved into the house next door to Viktor and Mary. My parent's garden wrapped around the back of Viktor's house so that it wasn't long before he and my father were having conversations over the garden fence. They were neighbours for nine years and became good friends. I remember one hot afternoon when my own two children, then of primary school age, were swimming in the outdoor pool in the garden and some friends had been invited along. In their excitement some of the girls were squealing loudly. I remember Mary calling over to me and asking the children to stop screaming because it was upsetting Viktor, which of course I did, but at that time had no idea of Viktor's background and why it had upset him so much.

Because my father is German, Viktor enjoyed practicing his German with him, and although my father is at least five years younger than Viktor they shared boyhood war experiences that were so different from the people in Britain. My parents did tell me that they had heard Viktor and Mary talk about an escape from Siberia and a long walk to Persia to join the British army. Of course, I thought it sounded as though it would make a good story but was told that Viktor didn't really want it talked about and only shared a few memories. For the next few years, I thought nothing more about it. My parents and I moved in together in a new property, about a fifty-minute drive distant, that would be suitable for me to look after them some time in the hopefully distant future. My parents continued to visit them several times a year and kept in touch by telephone.

Over the years since my childhood, my father had told many stories of his own adventures, particularly during WW2. In 2016 I decided it was time to make voice recordings of his memories and weave them into a book. I spent about two years on this project reading primary sources such as journals and air force records to be as historically accurate as I could be and establish a proper timeline. The book, covering just the war years, was published in 2018. My parents proudly took a copy to give to Viktor and Mary. In 2019, Mary told me that she had really enjoyed reading about my father as a boy and asked if I would after all write Viktor's story in the same way. Finally, Viktor agreed to it with the strict proviso and a solemn promise that I would not use his name in the book.

On August 21st of that year, I took my parents for tea and cakes with Viktor and Mary and took along my voice recorder. This was the first time I had heard the story from Viktor himself. There were a great many interruptions as sandwiches and cake was handed around, besides tea and coffee. My parents, already elderly themselves also interrupting with various items of family gossip. Back home, listening to the recording I realised how many questions I still had and arranged another visit, this time alone. By now it was October 11th, 2019. Viktor managed to answer some of my questions but was unable to recall many of the details and was extremely evasive about others. At various times during the interview, Mary would interrupt by saying “Well it’s all in the book”. Eventually I asked her what book she was referring to and she tottered out of the room coming back several minutes later with a bundle of typed A4 sheets. This ‘book’ had been typed on an old-fashioned mechanical typewriter and I was told that I would be allowed to photocopy it but must return the original as soon as possible. I was also shown a few photographs about which I was also sworn to secrecy.

Mary explained that in 1995, at which time she believed that Viktor was aged seventy, she had been offered surgery for a medical issue and had been warned that there was a small possibility that she might lose her sight. She persuaded Viktor to tell his story and she wrote it down in shorthand as he spoke, and later typed it up. As it turned out her eyesight was not affected, but now she had a written record of Viktor’s memoirs.

Having read through the ‘book’, I found I had more questions than answers and realised that I would have to do a great deal of background reading to fully understand the context of Viktor’s account going right back to 1914. After several months, often feeling that I was hitting a brick wall because I had no names for people or specific places, I finally decided that I would try to extract a name of some sort from Mary. By now we were into the early months of 2020, the country was in lockdown because of the COVID-19 global pandemic, and I couldn’t visit Mary to meet face to face. I made a telephone call, explaining that I was really finding it very difficult to do the background research for the book without any kind of name.

"Rewicz," she told me, slowly spelling it out. "His name was Rewicz, but he had to change it when he enlisted in the British army." We chatted for a bit, then I hung up feeling very positive about being able to verify a few facts – how wrong I was!

Straight away I googled the name Rewicz and up came the Slavomir Rawicz book 'The Long Walk'. I read the synopsis and then sat in stunned silence for several minutes trying to think what this meant. I rang Mary back.

"Mary, I have just made a quick internet search on the name you gave me. What do you know about the book 'The Long Walk?" I asked feeling utterly bewildered.

"Oh yes," she replied casually, "I read it when it was first published in the 1950s."

"But what about the similarities?" I asked, "The same name?" (Vowels by the way seem to be interchangeable).

"It's just a coincidence," was the rather surprising reply. "Lots of people escaped from Siberia," she added with the intention of being helpful.

I now felt obliged to explore this book, 'The Long Walk', that seemed to have become widely known, and then discovered that a book had been written about the original book, called 'Looking for Mr Smith', there had even been a movie made of the story, called 'The Way Back', and the BBC had made a documentary. At this point I felt like Alice in Wonderland, as if I had fallen down a rabbit hole into a whole other world.

As I continued my own research, I read numerous journals and memoirs of other Poles who had been deported to Siberia or imprisoned by the Soviets. In my search for the name Rawicz, I found little that was helpful, only more questions. For instance, there were several high-ranking officers in the Polish Army, and later in the Polish underground army (the AK), interrogated by the NKVD, who used the name Rawicz as a nom de guerre. Rawicz was also the name of a Polish military cadet school. Viktor, having kept the secret of his and his father's identities in spite of torture and other nameless horrors, including decades of fear of discovery by the NKVD (later the KGB), and having suffered brain damage and memory loss, may now simply be unable to recall names even if he wished to.

I have included Mary's transcript and transcripts of my own interviews so that the reader can judge for themselves the veracity of the story. When I first began talking to Viktor, it seemed to me that the extreme secrecy which he felt the need to maintain was unnecessary and bordering on paranoid, but consider this extract taken from the preamble to a ruling by the Court of Human Rights May 14th, 2013, providing the background information of the 'Public Security Authorities' – the Polish communist secret police apparatus that operated between 1944-1990:

"The apparatus, which was reshaped several times, consisted of different services and institutions, comprising the political police and special armed forces. It was patterned on the NKVD, i.e. the Soviet People's Commissariat for Internal Affairs) and the KGB, i.e. the Committee for State Security) and established (under the supervision of the NKVD) in 1944 with a view to

securing Communist rule and combating, suppressing, and eliminating groups of political opposition, including the post-war underground resistance against Communism and the Polish Church. In the 1950s these organs were in charge of prisons and labour camps; at that time, they were also competent to conduct criminal investigations under the rules of criminal procedure (see Domalewski v. Poland (dec.), no. 4610/97, ECHR 1999-V).

From 1956 onwards, when the level and nature of repression changed, their tasks involved in the protection of the communist system included, among other things, the control and infiltration of Polish society secured by its own members and through a system of paid or unpaid informers and secret collaborators, denunciation, monitoring of persons in, or cooperating with, the opposition, political opponents, priests, and other persons suspected of being in any way associated with anti-communist ideas or critical of the communist party's programme, its role, and members."

Phrases such as 'eliminating groups of political opposition' speak for themselves. The evidence here certainly leads me to conclude that Viktor's fears were well founded.

Finding documentary evidence has been almost impossible. I do not speak Polish, I do not have any names to follow up, and shortly before the pandemic, the Russian Human Rights group 'Memorial' was shut down. I have seen, although I wasn't allowed to photograph it, a commemorative certificate from the Italian campaign that clearly has Viktor's name; it is the same name that he married under in England in 1951. I have also found a public record of this marriage to Mary in 1951. I can verify that Viktor and Mary were married in Worcestershire, England in 1951 and that Viktor served in the Polish Second Corps under that name. The National Archives at Kew hold a record of Viktor's Naturalisation Certificate issued March 19th, 1963, which I have seen; paperwork that he would have required for his visit to his mother in Poland that year. At the same time, I have not found any documentary evidence to contradict anything what Viktor has told me, rather the memoirs and journals of others seem to corroborate his story.

From the outset, Viktor, and Mary both insisted that if I were to write his story, using Mary's 'book' as the basis, plus a few interview recordings, that I must on no account use his name. His father apparently changed his name after the revolution and Viktor has done the same. Having signed the Official Secrets Act, he is of course obliged to maintain his silence on some subjects. I have no reason to doubt that everything that Viktor has told me or his wife, has been what he believed to be true.

www.ingramcontent.com/pod-product-compliance
Lightning Source LLC
La Vergne TN
LVHW030921080826
845145LV00013B/3001

* 9 7 8 1 9 1 3 9 4 6 2 5 8 *